ANNA ZIEGLER: PLAYS ONE

T0347501

Anna Ziegler

PLAYS ONE

methuen | drama

LONDON • NEW YORK • OXFORD • NEW DELHI • SYDNEY

METHUEN DRAMA
Bloomsbury Publishing Plc
50 Bedford Square, London, WC1B 3DP, UK
1385 Broadway, New York, NY 10018, USA
29 Earlsfort Terrace, Dublin 2, Ireland

BLOOMSBURY, METHUEN DRAMA and the Methuen Drama logo
are trademarks of Bloomsbury Publishing Plc

First published in Great Britain by Oberon Books 2016
This edition published by Methuen Drama 2022

A Delicate Ship © Anna Ziegler, 2016, *Boy* © Anna Ziegler, 2016,
The Last Match © Anna Ziegler, 2016 and *Photograph 51* © Anna
Ziegler, 2015.

Collection Copyright © Anna Ziegler, 2016
Introduction Copyright © Billy Carden, 2016

Cover design by James Illman

Anna Ziegler has asserted her right under the Copyright,
Designs and Patents Act, 1988, to be identified as author of this work.

A catalogue record for this book is available from the British Library.

A catalog record for this book is available from the Library of Congress.

ISBN: PB: 978-1-3503-5025-0
eBook: 978-1-7831-9316-5

Series: Modern Plays

To find out more about our authors and books visit www.bloomsbury.com
and sign up for our newsletters.

For my parents

Contents

Note

A slash (/) indicates overlapping dialogue.

Each play should be performed without an intermission.

Introduction

Luminous is a word that is often repeated in describing the plays of Anna Ziegler. And if you are ever fortunate enough to meet her you will get the sense of someone who is carrying a light within. In her gifted hands the stories she chooses to tell become acts of illumination in which she deconstructs the linear and expands our familiar and certain notions of time to quicken our sense of what it means to be alive.

In each of these four plays Anna is using what we could see as familiar stories if told in a linear way. *A Delicate Ship* is the story of a love triangle, two men competing for the same woman. *Photograph 51* is the well-known story of the British scientist Rosalind Franklin's betrayal by her male colleagues in their race to discover the structure of DNA. *Boy* is inspired by the real story of the misguided attempt to raise a child born a boy as a girl. And in *The Last Match* an aging tennis star is challenged by a young player on the rise. But instead of giving us the expected, Anna expands the world of each play to illuminate the larger mysteries and paradoxes that make us human.

To do this she dances with time in a unique and beguiling fashion. Her characters move backward and forward as they seek to understand who they are, who they were and who they will become. As Delmore Schwartz wrote:

> Time is the school in which we learn
> Time is the fire in which we burn.

So in these plays we see characters who have made irrevocable mistakes and how their attempts to comprehend their causes, results and consequences send them spinning through the dimensions of time.

In *A Delicate Ship*, Nate's answer to happiness is to "… traverse the endless series of days like explorers in a ship made of time itself, its delicate sails moving easily through the churning water." And later, when the violent moment comes that changes all their lives, Sarah says "Time was zig-zagging across the sky. It was earlier that night, it was earlier that week, it was the rest of our lives all at once." The epigraph for *Photograph 51* is a quote from Ann Patchett's novel *Run* that resonates throughout the play: "Certain things exist outside of time. It was ten years ago, it was this morning… It happened in the past and it was always happening. It happened every single minute of the day." A poem quoted in *Boy* notes that "Time is a thief," and Adam feels that years of his life have been stolen. In *The Last Match,* the aging champion Tim has these thoughts as he plays the most crucial point during the match: "…my feet are moving and my mind is in overdrive and there are a ton of stars above our heads and it's the middle of the night and it's the middle of my life only it's the end, and my son is already grown, and my parents have been gone many years and I am old: I am no longer a boy."

As you become familiar with these plays you realize that we order time in an attempt to understand our lives in a logical, linear way. But Anna opens the door into a more revealing world where time past is alive in time present and time present is alive in time future so who we are in any given moment is part of a larger, more beautiful chaos.

Anna is also a poet, but like Samuel Beckett and Harold Pinter who also wrote poetry, she is a playwright first—which means that what she writes are truly plays. She has a profound understanding that language is not just how we talk, but how we reveal ourselves to others and to ourselves. *A Delicate Ship* may be the most overtly poetic of her plays and *Boy* seemingly the least. But in each play the use of language is rigorously crafted and specific so that lines and words resonate beyond the immediate, allowing her characters to take us with them as they glimpse the undiscovered and unresolved within themselves.

Over seven years ago, Anna was introduced to us at the Ensemble Studio Theatre (EST) by our Director of New Play Development, Linsay Firman, and we have had the good fortune to work closely with Anna ever since. *Photograph 51* and *Boy* were developed through readings and workshops and then produced Off-Broadway by the EST/Alfred P. Sloan Foundation Project for science themed plays. *Boy* was presented in a partnership with the Keen Company. Both productions were beautifully directed by Linsay Firman.

Anna is a generous and exacting collaborator. From our experience of working with these two of her plays we have learned that the most important challenge in bringing them to the stage is achieving the right tone. The plays are like a light kid glove with a tough and stronger hand inside. So you need to achieve a dexterous balance that gives full life to their playfulness and humor, while sometimes masking and sometimes revealing the tougher hand within that is driving the action. In that sense the many moments of reflection are always active because as her characters may be living lightly in the present they are being driven by a certain turmoil within.

When I asked Linsay Firman about her experience directing these plays she wrote:

> Anna's writing is insightful and expansive, but also wonderfully funny and playful. She uses her plays to explore the largest and most basic human experiences—love, faith, failure and death—juxtaposed with the mundane, often comic, details of every day life. Directing Anna's work, I've come to appreciate how she uses that balance to make the largest ideas feel immediate, and the most trivial details feel profound. She writes with incredible empathy for her characters, despite, or perhaps because of, their flaws. She tempers heightened emotion with humor and she encourages her collaborators to do the same. She never wants the production or performances to underline the pathos, but rather to draw the audience in with the accessible humanity of her characters so that the larger questions and profound insights dawn gradually for those watching.

"I think someone sees something new each time one looks at beautiful things" says Rosalind Franklin in *Photograph 51*. This is true of Anna's plays as well. They are wholly original and careful constructs that emerge from a mind that knows the discoveries come from asking the questions, not from answering them. In *Photograph 51* as we watch scientists racing to discover the secret of life, we realize that the secret is bigger than the double helix; there is so much more we don't know about ourselves, our origins and the fact of our own mortality. The competition gives way to a deeper sense of wonder as with strange joy we seek to understand how and why human beings come to do what they do. That is the journey Anna strives to take us on in these plays and as we look at them again and again, the discoveries will only continue.

Billy Carden, 2016
Artistic Director,
Ensemble Studio Theatre, New York

A DELICATE SHIP

Characters

SARAH

early-mid 30s (sensitive and kind and indecisive, big-hearted with an easy laugh, the kind of woman who doesn't realize men are in love with her and struggles with fear in a way that makes her sidestep her life a little bit)

NATE

early-mid 30s (a deeply wounded poet-type, quick-witted and razor-sharp, with an epically ranging emotional scale; he is too smart for his own good, obsessed with his own self-hatred, but appreciative of honesty in any form)

SAM

early-mid 30s (a dreamer and former dork, the sweet guy you'd want your daughter to marry, who never wants to offend anyone; he is honest and smart, and tries very hard to fit in. He's also a musician who plays a guitar)

Setting

Nominally, an apartment in Brooklyn, on Christmas Eve. The present day. The play also occupies a memory space that exists before and after the night when the action of the play takes place.

A Delicate Ship was originally produced by Cincinnati Playhouse in the Park (Blake Robison, Artistic Director; Buzz Ward, Managing Director) on March 22, 2014. The director was Michael Evan Haney, the stage manager Becky Merold, the set designer Narelle Sissons, the costume designer Gordon DeVinney, the lighting designer Kirk Bookman, and the sound designer Fabian Obispo. The cast was as follows:

SARAH	Janie Brookshire
NATE	Karl Miller
SAM	Ben Diskant

The Off-Broadway premiere of *A Delicate Ship* was produced by The Playwrights Realm (Katherine Kovner, Artistic Director) on August 18, 2015. The director was Margot Bordelon, the stage manager Alyssa Howard, the set designer Reid Thompson, the costume designer Sydney Maresca, the lighting designer Nicole Pearce, and the composition and sound designer Palmer Hefferan. The cast was as follows:

SARAH	Miriam Silverman
NATE	Nick Westrate
SAM	Matt Dellapina

'I'm nostalgic for conversations I had yesterday. I've begun reminiscing events before they even occur. I'm reminiscing this right now.'

Noah Baumbach, *Kicking and Screaming*

'When I asked him why he had never married, he told me life had slipped away too quickly. Sensing he was being disingenuous, I later ventured to ask again. This time, quietly, almost in a whisper, he said his parents had been "twin souls," and he knew it would "always remain impossible to match what they had had."'

Dmitri Nabokov (Vladimir's son) to Lila Azam Zanganeh, as reported in her essay *His Father's Best Translator, The New York Times,* July 20, 2012

'And this is the simple truth - that to live is to feel oneself lost. He who accepts it has already begun to find himself, to be on firm ground. Instinctively, as do the shipwrecked, he will look around for something to which to cling, and that tragic, ruthless glance, absolutely sincere, because it is a question of his salvation, will cause him to bring order into the chaos of his life. These are the only genuine ideas; the ideas of the shipwrecked. All the rest is rhetoric, posturing, farce.'

Søren Kierkegaard

'I too am not a bit tamed, I too am untranslatable,
I sound my barbaric yawp over the roofs of the world.
The last scud of day holds back for me,
It flings my likeness after the rest and true as any on the shadow'd wilds,
It coaxes me to the vapor and the dusk.'

Walt Whitman, *Song of Myself*

"We must love one another or die."

(For a 1955 anthology text Auden changed this line to
"We must love one another and die" to circumvent what
he regarded as a falsehood in the original.)

W. H. Auden, *September 1, 1939*

About suffering they were never wrong,
The Old Masters; how well they understood
Its human position: how it takes place
While someone else is eating or opening a window or just
    walking dully along;
How, when the aged are reverently, passionately waiting
For the miraculous birth, there always must be
Children who did not specially want it to happen, skating
On a pond at the edge of the wood:
They never forgot
That even the dreadful martyrdom must run its course
Anyhow in a corner, some untidy spot
Where the dogs go on with their doggy life and the torturer's horse
Scratches its innocent behind on a tree.

In Breughel's Icarus, for instance: how everything turns away
Quite leisurely from the disaster; the ploughman may
Have heard the splash, the forsaken cry,
But for him it was not an important failure; the sun shone
As it had to on the white legs disappearing into the green
Water; and the expensive delicate ship that must have seen
Something amazing, a boy falling out of the sky,
had somewhere to get to and sailed calmly on.

W. H. Auden, *Musée des Beaux Arts*

Lights up on an almost bare stage. Three actors are arranged around it– SARAH and SAM sit together, and NATE stands a little apart from them. It is late in the evening, well after dinner. A Christmas tree sits undecorated in the middle of the room.

NATE: *(To the audience.)* They were discussing how consciousness emerges from suffering. He was arguing that:

SAM: You can only be truly self-aware when you're in pain.

SARAH: I disagree.

NATE: *(Drily and with obvious disdain.)* He was something of a philosophy nut. In college, he took both semesters of the Russian lit survey. You know, Doestoevsky, Gogol, Pushkin. That sort of thing got him going.

SAM: If you're happy, you're not thinking. Not really. Think about the happiest moments in your life. Are you analyzing them? No, you analyze the bad stuff. You relive the bad stuff over and over again.

SARAH: I analyze everything. I analyze the good stuff to make sure it's not actually bad.

NATE: It was snowing. That night.

(It snows.)

SARAH: This is Nate.

NATE: It was Christmas.

SARAH: This is years ago.

NATE: We grew up together. In an apartment building in the city at the center of the world. I lived just above her. 6A.

SARAH: 5A.

NATE: *(Wryly lewd.)* We had the same bedroom. Every night I slept on top of her.

SARAH: Nate still lives in that building. I mean, he doesn't, really. But he does.

(SAM turns to the audience.)

SAM: When I met Nate–

SARAH: Christmas, years ago now.

SAM: He knocked on the door. We weren't expecting him.

NATE: It was snowing.

SARAH: This was years ago.

NATE: Everything was years ago.

SAM: We were…

(SARAH and SAM kiss. Then he looks into her eyes.)

The last few months were almost too good to be true. Every night we stayed up so late talking that the next day I was in a fog of Sarah.

SARAH: I'd fall asleep in my chair at work. I'd sit with my back to the door so no one would see.

SAM: Every song I heard was suddenly about her. About us.

SARAH: There was something in his eyes that made me think of my dad. And that was nice.

SAM: *(A little abashed.)* I told her I loved her on our third date. *(Then, to her.)* I'd never said it to anyone before. Did you know that?

SARAH: *(Sadly.)* I didn't know that.

SAM: And then there was this knock.

(A knock on the door.)

SAM: Are you expecting someone?

SARAH: *(To the audience.)* What if we just hadn't opened the door? I sometimes get trapped in the loop of that question. To this day, it can take hours to get out of that loop.

(Another knock.)

SAM: Sarah?

SARAH: *(Calling out.)* Who is it?

NATE: It's me.

SAM: *(To SARAH.)* Who's me?

SARAH: *(Letting him in.)* Nate!

SARAH and NATE embrace.

NATE: Merry Christmas.

SARAH: *(Happily.)* What are you doing here?

> *SAM is hanging back, waiting to be introduced. NATE notices him.*

NATE: Your manners, Sarah.

SARAH: Oh, okay. Right. Nate—this is Sam.

SAM: Hey.

NATE: He doesn't know about me?

SARAH: *(A little warily.)* What are you doing here?

NATE: I was in the neighborhood.

SAM: *(To the audience.)* This wasn't true. He wasn't in the neighborhood.

NATE: *(To the audience.)* This is Sarah. She wouldn't want me to define her by what she does every day, even though what she does every day is perfectly interesting.

SARAH: *(To the audience.)* This is Sam. My boyfriend. He's a singer-slash-philosopher-slash-legal secretary. He's a paralegal who takes philosophy courses and is in a band. He thinks he's shy, but I think he's quiet. I like that he doesn't always have something he feels he has to say…And one day he'll be famous.

NATE: *(To the audience.)* But not yet.

SARAH: *(To NATE.)* Well, it's good to see you.

SAM: So how do you and Sarah…?

NATE: Me and Louise here?

SARAH: *(Not knowing how to explain.)* He calls me Louise.

SAM: Is that like a nickname?

NATE: Like a nickname.

SARAH: We had this class together and—

NATE: It's fucking freezing out there. I thought my ears were gonna fall off.

SARAH: Well, you should wear a hat. You never wear a hat.

NATE: *(Matter-of-fact.)* And the streets were empty, and the subway was empty. I think it was colder because everything was so empty.

SAM: Well, it's Christmas Eve.

NATE: I know.

SAM: Where are you coming from?

NATE: In what sense? Physically? Intellectually? Emotionally?

SARAH: Sorry — he's crazy.

NATE: Only for you.

SAM: So, did you guys go to college together, or?

SARAH: We grew up together.

SAM: Okay, awesome. Awesome.

> *A breath.*

SARAH: *(To NATE.)* Do you want a drink?

NATE: Would I ever turn down a drink?

SARAH: Well, are you staying?

NATE: What kind of question is that? I'm here, aren't I?

SARAH: For all I know you're just stopping by.

NATE: *(A little sharp/pointed.)* Aren't you happy to see me?

SARAH: I said I was.

NATE: *(To SAM.)* See, every Christmas Eve, we'd meet in the stairwell of our building. And we'd smoke a joint and gossip like old hens about everything–our friends and classmates, who was fucking who and how dreadful it must be to be them when of course all we wanted was to be them.

SARAH: Remember the year when one of the Jorges caught us — *(To SAM.)* our building had two supers both named Jorge –

NATE: It was the grouchy one. Grouchy Jorge.

SARAH: But he just sat down and was like, can I have a hit?

NATE: And then a couple weeks later, he got busted for dealing drugs to high-schoolers.

SARAH: *(That puts a damper on things.)* Oh yeah, I forgot that part.

(Amazed.) God, it all feels like such a long time ago. It's crazy.

NATE: *(Honest, serious.)* I didn't want to be on my own tonight, okay?

Beat. NATE and SARAH look at each other.

SAM: You know, Kierkegaard said that loneliness makes us poets.

NATE: What?

SAM: He said the only genuine ideas are the ideas of the shipwrecked. So, like, the best thinking, the clearest thinking, is done by people who are lost or suffering or lonely.

NATE: *(As in "where'd you find this guy?")* Who is this guy?

SARAH: He's my boyfriend.

NATE: *(Without snark.)* Your boyfriend.

SAM: I sort of–perversely, I know–but I like the idea that to live is to be lost. And that only when we accept that state of being lost, of being lonely, can we create some order in our lives.

NATE: You like that idea?

SAM: Yeah. I do.

NATE: Then you must not have experienced it.

SARAH: Nate–

NATE: You must never have really grieved in your life, really lost anything. Losses that big don't make us poets. The past doesn't disappear so that we can write about it.

SARAH: Nate lives in the past. Sometimes I have to go back there just to find him and drag him back here.

SAM: Some philosophers argue the past isn't real. Isn't that an incredible concept?

NATE: Hey, so I brought weed. Or we can keep talking about this stuff.

SAM: You brought dope?

NATE: Do you smoke dope?

SAM: Not in a long time, but...

NATE: Well, if you smoked it in the past and the past isn't real then...

SAM: It's really more figurative...

SARAH: Don't be a child, Nate.

NATE: I don't actually see why anyone would want to be anything but a child.

SARAH: Oh god, this is his theory–

NATE: It's not a theory. It's a statement about life. That the primary joys we experience are as children.

SARAH: I don't agree.

NATE: Because agreeing would be admitting your life is getting gradually but steadily worse and that's an existential predicament you do not wish to acknowledge.

SARAH: Probably. But who cares?

NATE: *(To SAM.)* So what have you heard about me exactly?

SAM: What do you mean?

NATE: I mean, have I come up in conversation?

SAM: *(To SARAH.)* Has he?

SARAH: *(To NATE, skeptically.)* Why do you ask?

SAM: To be honest, the last few months have been a bit of a blur.

NATE: A blur, huh.

SAM: But what should I know about you? Why don't you tell me.

SARAH: *(To the audience.)* I am tweed skirts and tall boots and insomnia. I am sleeping with the light on when I'm home alone. I am the woman reading The New Yorker on the subway, mostly the cartoons and the movie reviews and occasionally an essay about the failures of doctors and hospitals and how we could, all of us, die very young. I am hoping for so many things but assume I won't get any of them. In this memory, tonight, I am thirty-three. I am older than my mother was when she had me. And I have been alone a long time. I've had boyfriends but when you're thirty-three and not married and a woman, you've been alone a very long time. I still own cassette tapes. I'm a social worker but not particularly social. Nate is my best friend but I would never tell him so. Maybe I live in the past too.

NATE: And I come bearing more gifts. I bring you champagne—

> *He produces some from a bag.*

Voila.

SARAH: Nate—

NATE: And the biggest bag of Cheez Doodles I could find—

> *Out it comes.*

SARAH: *(Sarcastic.)* Reading my mind again.

NATE: Come on: deep inside, you know you love Cheez Doodles.

SARAH: Do I? Or did I say that once—once—when we were kids?

NATE: In 6th grade, you ate Cheez Doodles every Tuesday and Thursday on your way home from ballet in the car service with your mom. Then you got sick of them and we made up a No-More-Cheez-Doodles dance that we performed for my babysitter and her sister who was visiting from Barbados and you haven't had them since.

SARAH: How do you remember that.

NATE: And it wasn't long after you stopped eating Cheez Doodles that you stopped dancing.

SAM: I didn't know you used to dance.

SARAH: Yeah, I–

NATE: Once a dancer always a dancer. Like time: it happened, it's happening, it will happen, but all at once. The girl gallivanting around the city eating Cheez Doodles at the same time as the woman claims never to have liked them.

SAM: Well, they go well with pot.

NATE: I couldn't agree more.

SAM: So hey, do you mind if I?

> *He indicates the joint, and NATE hands it to him. Something changes; this next section is outside of time.*

NATE: And I bring you a memory.

SARAH: Of what?

NATE: Sophomore year of college. I'm visiting you during my spring break, and we sit out on blankets on the quad in front of your dorm, one of those beautiful medieval dorms so it feels like it could be four hundred years ago. The endless timeless life of the college is all around us, sunlight dappling people's backs as they lie out on blankets, and also the people who laid out right here fifteen years ago, and forty. Our parents are out here on blankets too, young, and they know nothing of what's ahead.

SARAH: Our parents?

NATE: Well, they're always there, if we are. In a sense.

SARAH: I guess–

NATE: It breaks my heart it's so beautiful. The idea that one day we'll have children and when we do they will just seem... inevitable. But that there was also a point–most of our lives, really–when we didn't know them at all, weren't sure they would even come to be. But all along there they were, inside of us, singing.

SARAH: I don't know that I'll have children.

NATE: Oh no, you will.

SARAH: How do you know that?

NATE: In this memory, it's April and we're reading the *Sunday Times*, which takes most of the afternoon. It's one of those days that lasts forever and goes so quickly. And at the end of it, I am holding your toes in my hand–

SARAH: I don't remember that.

NATE: I am. I am holding your toes. You were wearing flip-flops but then your feet got cold because it was getting dark and the day was going away. You were cold and so I held your feet in my hands.

SARAH: My feet.

NATE: And your toes. Everything I could.

SARAH: Okay.

NATE: And then I told you I loved you.

    A breath.

SARAH: And what did I say?

NATE: What do you think?

SARAH: I think I said…I love you too.

NATE: So you do remember.

    A soft shift back to the present.

SAM: *(Finishing a toke.)* Okay. Okay. So, like, who are you?

NATE: "I'm nobody, who are you? Are you nobody too? Then there's a pair of us. Don't tell. They'd banish us you know."

SARAH: *(To the audience.)* No. Nate is a dancer. A writer. A tight-rope walker. A man on stilts. He is always ready with a joke. Always ready with a gin and tonic. Always ready with the right words. With elaborate plans and epic poems. For a long time, I assumed he was gay.

NATE: I'm not.

SARAH: I was wrong. Who is Nate? I don't know. He's none of those things, really, and also all of them. During the day,

17

he teaches third grade. But he wants to be an artist. No one is better with third graders than Nate but he's the saddest third grade teacher I know.

NATE: I came by because I was in the neighborhood and I wanted to give you this poem. I found a xeroxed copy of it tucked inside a diary from 1993.

SARAH: What were you doing looking at a diary from 1993??

SAM: I kept a diary in high school.

SARAH: You did?

SAM: Yeah, and I remembered it being really deep, like really profound, but I read it again recently and it's just filled with lines from *Clerks.*

SARAH: Oh god, I hated that movie!

NATE: I've always been sentimental. When I was seven I think I missed being four–

SARAH: If sentimental's another word for extremely weird.

NATE: Hey now. I think I'm going to have to have a little talk with your mother about your manners, Louise.

SAM: Too bad–you just missed her.

NATE: Cynthia Gloria Steinem Winthrop was here?? Tonight?

SARAH: I made dinner.

SAM: Was she a feminist or something?

SARAH: No. She went to a march–once. In like 1971. And for some reason Nate has this thing…

NATE: You made dinner? What, scrambled eggs and spaghetti?

SAM: Roast turkey. It was amazing.

NATE: Excuse me? You roasted a turkey? Like an actual bird that once lived and breathed?

SARAH: I cook, Nate. I do. All the time.

SAM: And then out of nowhere Sarah was like "a tree! We need a tree!" It was adorable.

NATE: So adorable. So the three of you went out and got that tree?

SAM: And those guys are just sitting out on the curb, freezing. No one's buying anything, and they're pissed they have to work on Christmas eve.

NATE: You must have made their night.

SAM: They carried it back here for us. Up the five flights of stairs. They're, like, my new favorite people.

SARAH: My mom kept saying, "if your father were here, this wouldn't be happening." Remember how he had to carry the tree by himself? Even when they stopped selling them on the corner and we had to go down to 86th Street.

NATE: It's called being a man.

SAM: I'm secure enough to let another man carry my tree.

NATE: *(A real question; the first moment of real tension.)* Are you?

SARAH: Of course he is.

> *She puts her arms around SAM.*

Some people don't go around assuming that everyone else is judging their masculinity every second.

NATE: Yeah: women.

SARAH: Nate.

NATE: So what do you make of Sarah's mother?

SAM: Cynthia? She's great. She's super nice.

NATE: So you haven't met her.

SARAH: My mother is nice!

NATE: Your mother has a temper, and laughs too loud, and is always looking for a bargain. She's the most sincere person I know. She's nice, but she's not nice. It's not how I'd define her.

SAM: You didn't let me finish.

NATE: When we were kids we had all these made up names for each other. But really, they were our parents. Everyone we pretended to be was some version of our parents. We thought they had perfect lives.

SARAH: We created this whole imaginary world together.

NATE: It wasn't imaginary.

SARAH: It was called–

NATE: No, that's private–

SAM: I don't need to know. It's okay.

SARAH: I had a Breugel poster in my room, of the Tower of Babel, and we decided we lived there, inside of it. We had a password–

NATE: Don't tell him that.

SARAH: Why, are you worried he'll break in??

NATE: Yes!

SARAH: Anyway, when one of us said the password, it meant we were there, suddenly, no matter where we were–school, or home. Anywhere.

NATE: We were there. In this castle, encircled by fields on one side and the sea on the other. Where it was very beautiful. And very quiet.

SAM: So what would you do there?

NATE: Do?

SARAH: Talk. We would just talk, for hours.

And feel less alone.

She and NATE share a moment.

NATE: One time Sarah's mom asked when we'd outgrow it, our world–

SARAH: And Nate said never. Which was–

NATE: Accurate. But it made Cynthia laugh–too loud. She said, "just you wait. We outgrow everything." But I disagree. I still disagree.

SAM: It's funny that I haven't heard about you.

NATE: Sarah's dad was also a really marvelous person.

SAM: I bet he was. I wish I'd met him–known him.

NATE: He was so much fun. Sometimes my mother would say he was too much. And I'd say "too much of what?" and she'd say "no, just too much, too much" and she was always laughing about him. Sometimes I think my mother might have had a thing for your father.

SARAH: She didn't.

NATE: I saw the way she looked at him.

SARAH: No. You're wrong.

NATE: And she liked the way he pronounced certain words. Like…

(To SAM.)

Say r-o-o-m.

SAM: Why?

NATE: Come on.

SAM: Fine. Room.

NATE: Right. And he would say rum. Like, "go to your rum, Sarah." No wonder she became an alcoholic.

SARAH: I am not an alcoholic.

SAM: She's not. I can barely get her tipsy.

NATE: Then you must not know the same Sarah I know…I was at my parents' tonight and they were like "it's true that no one knows you better than Sarah." And they were tangled up in each other on the couch, and I was, I admit, a little grossed out. I mean, it's intolerable how affectionate they still are with each other–

SARAH: I think it's nice.

NATE: And then I realized that they didn't need me anymore. I wasn't part of their little club. And they looked so old all of a sudden. I couldn't bear it…I mean, you can't hold onto anything, not anything. Not even your parents…Especially your parents.

SARAH: That's crazy. They need you.

SAM: I like that my parents don't need me.

NATE: And to make matters worse, without any warning, it became this, like, intervention. I didn't see it coming.

SAM: *(Matter-of-factly.)* I think that's generally how interventions work.

NATE: Oh yeah? Are they covered in intro philosophy classes these days?

SAM: Whoa.

SARAH: Nate.

> *(A breath.)*

NATE: *(Slowly, genuinely.)* I'm sorry. That was out of line. I'm sorry.

SARAH: Why don't you just give me the poem. The one you came to give me.

> *(He takes it from his back pocket and gives it to her.)*

NATE: It's about how everything disappears. And it made me think of you.

SARAH: *(Sarcastic.)* Gosh, thanks.

NATE: No, it's beautiful. If you had a beautiful loft apartment with a huge window overlooking the river and you could see the boats on the river with their little lights twinkling and it was Christmas Eve every night of the year and every night lasted forever–that's what this poem is like. But you don't have that apartment. So I knew you needed the poem. And I brought it to you.

> *(SARAH looks at him strangely.)*

SARAH: Are you okay, Nate?

NATE: I'm more than okay.

SARAH: *(Unconvinced.)* Okay.

NATE: I'm very glad to be finally meeting Sam. I've heard a lot about you, after all.

SAM: Yeah?

NATE: We talk everyday.

SARAH: More like every couple weeks.

NATE: Every couple weeks but it feels like every day. Until pretty recently, it was every day. But lately, whenever I suggest we get together, she changes the subject. How do you like that. So what choice do I have but to come over here, with my Yuletide joint and my tail between my legs.

SARAH: I don't change the subject. I mean, we just saw each other, like…I don't know. I feel like we just saw each other.

> *Breath.*

SAM: Sorry, I'm a little…I'm sort of…I mean, is he like…did you guys go out, or something?

NATE: Oh no, it's much more serious than that.

SARAH: No, we never went out.

SAM: Okay, so just…like…okay.

NATE: Do you two need a moment?

SARAH: *(Not unkindly.)* You know, it's late, and…*(to NATE, quietly)* why don't we just talk tomorrow, okay?

SAM: No, it's fine. I just…I want to be in the loop, you know? He doesn't have to leave. I just…

SARAH: Are you sure?

SAM: Yeah. Of course. Just don't…

SARAH: Don't what?

SAM: Assume I know stuff. That's all.

SARAH: Of course. Of course not. I'm sorry.

SAM: It's fine. I don't mean to…I mean, it's fine. When we're married, I just don't want to find out you have an identical twin or something.

> *Beat.*

SARAH: *(Quietly but a little thrown.)* What?

SAM: What?

SARAH: Sam.

SAM: What?

SARAH: Nothing.

>*A breath.*

SAM: Oh—no—it just came out. Ignore it. It wasn't a proposal or anything.

SARAH: Okay...

SAM: Which isn't to say I think we won't get married one day.

SARAH: You think, um...?

SAM: Don't you?

>*She exits; NATE's very relaxed all of a sudden. SAM sits. An awkward silence.*

NATE: So are you from around here, or?

SAM: What?

NATE: You seem like you're from out west maybe. Like California.

>*Beat.*

Oh!...Is it Oregon? I'm getting kind of a Portland vibe.

>*Beat.*

And you write songs?

SAM: Yeah, I write songs.

NATE: What are they about?

SAM: I don't know.

>*SARAH enters, holding a box of ornaments.*

SARAH: They're about romance, of course.

NATE: If I wrote songs, they'd be about loneliness. And about the past.

SARAH: That's why it's good you don't write songs.

NATE: Ouch.

SARAH: Sam's songs are very sexy.

NATE: Is that right?

SARAH: That's right.

NATE: Do you want to sing one?

SAM: Not right now.

SARAH: How about we decorate the tree.

NATE: Your ornaments suck. No offense.

SARAH: No they don't.

SAM: We're Jewish, but we used to get a tree anyway. My parents would put Jewish stars all over it. Which I always thought was weird. Like if you're gonna be one thing be that thing. If you want to be something else be that other thing.

SARAH: I don't know. I think it's sweet. Not to feel you have to choose.

SAM: Well, one year I made an ornament out of popsicle sticks at school and it looked like a big cross. But I didn't mean for it to be a big cross. I was just fucking around and I didn't know anything. And my parents were too nice not to use it. So at our holiday party, they had all their friends over and there was this big cross on our tree. I remember my mom's friend Susan Stern just staring at it, and like calling her husband over and pointing at it. I asked my parents about it later and they said Susan Stern was a serious Jew who didn't even approve of our having a tree and that what I made wasn't a cross even though it looked like one. They said everything is about intention, which I totally disagree with. I mean, I think people hurt each other without meaning to all the time. And the lack of intention doesn't mitigate the hurt.

NATE: What's a serious Jew?

SAM: At the time, I thought they meant she was a really serious person who happened to be Jewish.

NATE: That's a serious Jew. I agree.

SAM: But then I guess I realized she was someone who had firmer convictions about Judaism and God than I had— have—about anything.

NATE: *(Genuinely surprised.)* Wow. You are surprisingly honest.

SARAH: Sam is incredibly honest. And he's funny. And his music is…Well, one day everyone will know it. I really believe that.

NATE: Are we writing this guy's online dating profile or having an evening? I vote for having an evening.

SARAH: *(To NATE.)* Maybe we should write your online dating profile.

NATE: Man, she's tough, isn't she. When she doesn't want you to think she likes you back.

SAM: You're telling me.

NATE: I say we decorate that tree. Instead of writing something I have no use for.

SAM: If only we had popsicle sticks. I'd make an even better cross. I'd decorate it with sayings. Things my girlfriends have said that I'll never forget.

SARAH: What have they said?

SAM: One told me my Adam's Apple was too prominent. Another told me I have thin wrists.

SARAH: You don't. You have wonderful wrists.

NATE: Men and our insecurities. Everything is an affront to one's manhood. Everything. Women don't understand how hard it is to be a man. How hard it is not to cry sometimes.

SAM: One told me I shouldn't be in a band. That I'm not a "natural performer."

NATE: Can you sing?

SARAH: He sings beautifully.

NATE: Then you should be in a band. If I could sing…

SARAH: We used to make up songs. And then sing them for our parents.

NATE: To annoy them. But really to make them love us.

SAM: Another one walked away when I said I thought I'd marry her.

Beat.

Doesn't that just take the cake?

NATE: I think it might take the whole pantry. I think the kitchen is burning into the fucking ground.

SAM: I know, right?

SARAH: Sam, can we talk for a minute?

SAM: Another one told me I'd never grow up.

NATE: That's a good thing.

SAM: Not when your girlfriend says it.

NATE: I've never had a girlfriend. Been pining away for this one all my life.

SARAH: That's not true.

SAM: You've never had a girlfriend?

SARAH: He has. He's had plenty of girlfriends.

NATE: No one I really loved.

SARAH: Oh, you didn't love Nina Rothschild? You were obsessed with her.

NATE: Nina was hot and she didn't like me. So yeah sure I loved her. But I didn't love her. I don't use that word lightly.

SAM: Neither do I. I haven't loved very many people at all. In my life.

SARAH: Sam…

NATE: *(To the audience, or himself; subtle, matter-of-fact.)* There is some part of me that believes I can still be saved. That wants to be saved.

SAM: *(To the audience.)* The first time I saw Sarah was almost a year ago. She was sitting on a bench in the lobby of the building where I work. She was crying. She was incredibly beautiful and all alone. I wanted to go to her. I didn't. I went up in the elevator and sat at my desk and all day bad songs ran through my head.

NATE: If I wrote songs, they'd be about my parents…In some ways, this is a love song to our parents.

SARAH: Our lives are a love song to our parents.

SAM: The next day, she was there again, this time with an empty box perched on her lap. Again I didn't go to her. After that, I forgot about her; I mean, there was no reason to think I'd ever see her again.

SARAH: I always thought my parents loved each other so much.

NATE: I used to imagine them in college, meeting. Both wearing turtlenecks. My mother carrying a cello on her back. It's always autumn in this memory that I've created, and a bit chilly, and my father offers to carry her cello.

SAM: But then, a few months later, there she is, in the elevator. She's holding a box full of files and, like, framed photographs, and for a second I think I actually know her, like maybe we went to camp together or something? And I'm just, like, "hey."

SARAH: He was like "hey" and I sort of smiled and looked away the way you do when you don't know someone and they're talking to you. And then he said, "I'm sorry you were sad."

SAM: I didn't say that.

SARAH: You did. You said, "I'm sorry you were sad."

SAM: No it was probably like "Hey, um…I saw you a few months ago, here, in the lobby, and you looked upset, and, like, I'm sorry."

I'm not saying it wasn't totally a weird thing to say, but it wasn't just, like, without any context.

SARAH: Yes it was. And I loved that.

NATE: My father carries my mother's cello around the university, around the small city that houses the university, and they walk in circles, around and around, until they know everything there is to know about each other, and by that time it's night and no longer autumn, and they've had a child, and he is grown, and he is a source of sadness for them when once they were happy, walking in circles, on this autumn-y autumn-y day when they didn't know what was to come.

SARAH: Of course we went out. I mean, if someone remembers you in that way, if his memory of you is so generous and empathic, of course you go out.

NATE: At the same time, I can't bear the idea that one day they will just not be here anymore. I mean, what do you do, how can you go on, when the people whose dream you are are gone? After all, our dreams die with us, don't they? Sometimes I think I can't live another day, knowing what could—what will—happen.

SARAH: Why didn't you tell me that? Why didn't you ever articulate that to me??

NATE: I don't know.

SARAH: *(Angry, almost teary.)* No, that's not good enough.

SAM: For a second, before I opened my mouth in that elevator, I thought I knew her. Like we'd been friends at some point, long ago. That I knew her and she knew me. And it's good I did because it gave me the courage to speak. So I guess I'm glad memory works in such messed up ways.

NATE: *(Unimpressed.)* Who is this guy?? Memory works in "messed up ways."

SAM: I'm a Mets fan—always have been, die-hard—even during the years when they were worse than awful. I love sushi, though I didn't have the nerve to try it til I was thirty-two years old. I watched *Monty Python* and the *Holy Grail* over and over again in 8th grade, which also happened to be the year my parents split up.

I sometimes wonder why we can't just choose to be happy. I mean, it seems like we should reserve feeling bad for when truly bad things happen…but we don't.

(He takes a moment to think.)

I wrote my first song on a plane from Seattle to New Jersey, during a lightning storm. It was one of those days at the very end of summer when you feel like so much time is behind you.

I'd just been dumped by my college girlfriend. See, I was never good with girls…Sometimes I think you might spend your whole life trying to undo what you felt as a child.

SARAH: We went on a date.

SAM: Can I ask…like, what you were doing in my building? I mean, you don't work there, do you?

SARAH: No, I don't work there. I'm a social worker. I pay house calls to elderly people. I fill out the necessary forms for them. I help them find their hat or their wallet or their wives. They've lost so much it's often hard to decide what to look for.

SAM: So what were you…

SARAH: My father worked in that building. At first I couldn't bring myself to go up to his office. But then, eventually, I could. When I was a kid, he'd take me to work with him, all the way up to the 59th floor. And I'd never want to go home. I mean, all those windows. As though you were looking out on not just the city but the history of the city. All the time that was passing around you like a river. As though you could stay perched above all that time, and it wouldn't touch you…

NATE: Sarah's father was marvelous.

SAM: I bet.

SARAH: *(To the audience.)* He died. In January. And the world was filled with…no, emptied out. It was emptied out. We stood outside in the cemetery upstate and the ground was frozen that they…They lowered him into this frozen ground and I couldn't save him.

NATE: I was there. I thought: I'll save you. Sarah.

SARAH: The night of the funeral I had a dream that felt incredibly real. It was like I was a child again. My father was standing at the door of our apartment, waiting. He was always ready to go well before my mom or me; he'd stand there, holding a suitcase and pretending to scowl.

"You ladies are gonna be the death of me," he'd say, and then he'd tap his foot impatiently, in this exaggerated way, but he would always wait. In the dream, though–he left without us. The door opened and shut, and he was gone.

SAM: We had a great first date, didn't we? Like an epic kind of…like one of those first dates you thought happened only in movies.

SARAH: We did. We really did.

NATE: Oh yeah?

SAM: Yeah. It went on for hours. We had this tangible…It was intense.

SARAH: *(To the audience, wistful.)* During it, under an enormous night sky, I thought: I will marry this man. I really did.

SAM: *(To the audience, a humbling admission.)* And she looked so beautiful. And I forgot for a moment, for a few moments, that I was shy.

> *A breath.*

NATE: Let's play a game.

SARAH: No.

NATE: Come on, let's.

SARAH: I said no.

SAM: What kind of game?

NATE: Good. It's settled then.

SAM: What's the game?

NATE: Did you know Sarah was a Jeopardy wiz? She claims she hates games, but she was actually on Jeopardy.

SAM: No way.

NATE: Way. And what was the question that did you in? It had something to do with…No, I remember–

SARAH: I hate you, Nate.

NATE: Mythology, final Jeopardy: We often wax nostalgic about this young man who flew too close to the sun.

SAM: You didn't know that one?

SARAH: I blanked. I kept thinking of the father's name. I wrote it even though I knew it was wrong.

NATE: We often do things even though we know they're wrong. Just watch third graders in action. You can see the moral dilemma play out on their faces before they do whatever it was they were going to do in the first place.

SAM: I can't believe you were on Jeopardy.

NATE: She didn't tell you?

SARAH: It was in college; it was nothing.

NATE: It wasn't nothing. I watched with Sarah's parents. The three of us sat together in the studio audience, digging our nails into our palms whenever Sarah buzzed. Don't get it wrong, we all prayed. Don't get it wrong.

SARAH: Glad you had such faith in me.

NATE: More than Icarus should have had in his wings.

SARAH: Nate was like my third parent.

NATE: If you wanna sleep with your parents. But I think that's weird. Anyway: the game. We need supplies—pens and post-it notes.

SARAH: No. I hate that one. I hate anything that involves supplies.

NATE: Come on, Sarah. Lighten up.

SAM: Sarah can get a little testy.

NATE: You're telling me.

SARAH: You're both complete assholes. You know that?

SAM: Let's just play.

SARAH: Why do I feel like this is a terrible idea?

NATE: But we'll do it anyway. I like to call it the forehead game but really it's about getting to be someone else, or not knowing who you are. See, we each come up with a person, and stick it on someone else's forehead. Then each person has to figure out their identity. We take turns asking questions. The first one to guess right, wins.

SAM: Yes or no questions?

NATE: Oh no. That would be tedious.

SARAH: I find games tedious.

NATE: Like I said: that's a total lie.

SARAH: It's not, really.

NATE: She's a wiz at Boggle too. You should see how fast her mind works. She can pick out ten words in like ten seconds. Really impressed the kids growing up. That's why she was so popular. Well, with a sort of dorky crowd. Not that they didn't have their own hierarchy and their own cruelties.

SAM: What was Sarah like as a kid?

SARAH: Okay, let's not–

NATE: Marvelously human. Her fear and her hope lived right on the surface, like moss winding around a sapling. She always had to be holding someone's hand. Not just to cross the street. Always. Sometimes it was my hand. I can still feel it, her hand in mine.

SARAH: *(Quietly, humbled at the memory.)* That's bullshit.

NATE: And there were some shirts she would only wear inside-out. And if you tried to get the price tag sticker off her trapper keeper she shrieked like there was no tomorrow. She was weird, basically, and very loveable.

SAM: She have lots of friends?

NATE: Oh, lots of friends. But also none.

SARAH: That's you. You're describing yourself. I had lots of friends.

NATE: At her birthday parties, the magician or the storyteller or the balloon man would always look around, overwhelmed, and say "wow, there really are a lot of you, aren't there…" Those were fabulous parties.

SAM: And I bet she loved it. All that attention.

NATE: Our Louise doesn't mind a little attention.

SARAH: Are we gonna play this fucking game or not?

SAM: Am I sensing some frustration?

SARAH: Stop it, Sam.

NATE: I love this. We're all acting like little children. It's kind of adorable. A perfect setting for our game. Sarah, do you have post-its?

SARAH: I have post-its.

NATE: Get them.

> *She opens a drawer, retrieves the post-its and hands them out.*

SARAH: Okay.

NATE: Okay, everyone write down a name. Could be someone famous. Just has to be someone the person would know. I'll write for Sarah. Sam, you can do one for me, and Sarah you do Sam.

SARAH: Don't mind if I do. Do him.

> *No one laughs.*

Oh come on. Come on, Sam. Please just…

SAM: Just what?

NATE: Don't worry: this is how she gets. The major holidays have always put her on edge.

SARAH: What are you talking about?

NATE: We're all most conscious of our unhappiness on those days when we're supposed to be happy.

SAM: Yeah, come to think of it, I'm pretty conscious of mine right now.

NATE: Just write a name for god's sakes. Life is a series of tiny steps down a huge ladder at the bottom of which is the boiling abyss of death so we have to entertain ourselves while we're on this rickety fucking ladder or we'll start looking down and once you look down the dizziness might throw you right off.

SAM: That's great. That's really super.

NATE: Write! My god, don't you ever hear that voice in your head? A verb and an exclamation point and you have to do whatever it says. You just have to do it.

SAM: No. I don't hear that voice.

NATE: Well fucking write anyway.

>   *They write; SARAH is stuck.*

SARAH: I can't think of anyone.

NATE: *(In an accent.)* You can do it, Pauline. Then will you pass the peas?

SARAH: Fine. If only to stop you doing funny voices.

NATE: *(In another odd voice.)* Oh, it'll only make that worse.

SARAH: *(Writing something.)*

Okay. Happy now?

NATE: Is that a serious question?

SARAH: Nope.

NATE: I'm teasing you, darling.

>   *Then, genuine.*

Please just tolerate me. Please. I know it's hard.

SARAH: It's only hard when you make it hard.

NATE: Now, on the count of three, we all stick on the names. Ready? One...Two...Three.

>   *They do. On NATE: Jesus Christ. On SAM: Derek Jeter. On SARAH: Sarah.*

NATE: Sarah, you start.

SARAH: Fine.

>   *She thinks.*

Am I alive?

>   *SAM and NATE look at each other; there's a hint of a smile between them.*

NATE: Yes. Now you, Sam.

SAM: Okay. Am I alive?

NATE: Yes.

SARAH: Yes.

NATE: Same question. Am I among the living or the dead?

SAM: Dead.

SARAH: Well, sort of.

SAM: Yes. According to the majority of the world. Dead.

NATE: So I am living and dead.

SARAH: In a sense.

NATE: Am I the undead? Am I one of those vampires in those popular books for teenage girls?

SARAH: No. But some teenage girls do like you.

NATE: I'm like a teen idol?

SAM: In certain parts of the country.

SARAH: Too many answers for one go. My turn.

NATE: Those were all follow-up questions.

SARAH: All of these are follow-up questions. Am I a man?

SAM: No.

NATE: Okay, you go.

SAM: Fine, am I a man?

NATE: Very much so. A manly manly man. A man who never cries.

SARAH: Why doesn't anyone ever ask if they're a woman?

SAM: You didn't either.

SARAH: I know. It's horrible.

NATE: So am I popular with a more mature crowd too?

SAM: I'd say so.

NATE: Would you. Does Sarah like me?

SAM: Not particularly. Well, actually I'm not totally sure.

NATE: If I knew who it was I could tell you precisely whether or not Sarah liked him.

SARAH: Okay, enough. Am I a woman around my own age?

NATE: How do you like that–so you are.

SARAH: Whatever you're up to, Nate–quit it.

NATE: I'm not up to anything.

SAM: Am I famous?

SARAH: Yes.

NATE: Can't anyone ask an interesting question?? Jesus Christ.

> *SAM and SARAH look at each other.*

What?

> *Beat.*

Oh lord have mercy, am I Jesus Christ?

> *They nod.*

So I died for your sins. Remember that, people.

SARAH: Now he's going to lose interest in the game because he won.

SAM: *(Taking out his guitar and losing interest in the game.)* Isn't the game over because he won?

NATE: No, you have to figure out who you are.

SAM: I'm not sure I want to know.

NATE: Who are you Sarah?

SARAH: *(Gazing at SAM, while he plays.)* I'm in love.

SAM: I'm famous. Well, one day. And it doesn't feel at all the way I thought it might.

SARAH: I'm my parents. Cut in half and then multiplied. I'm there with them in the 70s, while they fall in love. They don't know I am, but I am. I watch. I try to see the future, but I can't make it out.

SAM: I sing.

(Taking out his guitar and beginning to play and sing.)

On the way to Washington where you live
I read about a man
who didn't feel
he was alive;
he walked through his days
wondering when he would be born
only to realize
he'd lived his whole life.

On the way to Washington where you live
I read about a man
who was sure
he would die;
they say he weathered the storm
of his own death too soon
and now he doesn't know what to do
with himself, being alive.

NATE: *(Interrupting.)* Come on. The game.

SAM continues to play, without singing.

SARAH: Hold on.

NATE: Why?

SARAH: I'm listening.

NATE: To that?

SAM stops playing abruptly.

SAM: Wait a second—you're not the guy who…No—Sarah, this isn't the guy who got so wasted he barfed on your friend's shoes while he was hitting on her at some high school party?

NATE: *(Quietly.)* You told him about that?

SARAH: *(Looking down.)* I don't know. It's a funny story.

SAM: This is that guy?? Shoe barf guy? No way. So I did hear about you, after all.

NATE: Well, just to be clear I wasn't hitting on her friend.

SAM: No?

NATE: I was hitting on her.

SARAH: No you weren't.

NATE: It's amazing how memory recreates things.

SARAH: It is amazing.

NATE: Just guess. Please.

SARAH: …Fine. Am I famous.

SAM: No.

NATE: Only to me.

SARAH: Oh god, am I some obscure poet or something? *(To SAM.)* Did he do one I'll never get?

SAM: I don't know if you'll get it.

NATE: Oh god, guess, will you?

SAM: Am I American?

NATE: Yes. Next.

SARAH: Am I American?

NATE: Jesus, these questions. Sarah, ask about your biggest fear. Or your greatest desire.

SARAH: No.

SAM: It's my turn anyway.

NATE: We could skip your turn.

SARAH: Nate!

SAM: So am I famous for some great achievement?

NATE: No.

SARAH: Yes. For a series of consistently great achievements.

NATE: But he asked if it was a single one.

SARAH: I know what he was trying to ask.

SAM: So I'm like an actor or an athlete or something.

NATE: Or something.

SARAH: No, that's right. You're an athlete.

> *She runs her fingers through SAM's hair or some other affectionate gesture that drives NATE crazy.*

NATE: Now you, Sarah. Ask if you're happy!

SARAH: Am I happy?

NATE: No!

SAM: I think so. More or less. / Most of the time.

NATE: And your biggest fear is of losing yourself. Losing yourself to the wrong choices, the wrong men, the wrong jobs, the wrong activity on a summer evening when whatever you're not doing is surely more fun. You know you let your brain lead your heart and you worry this won't make you happy in the end, but losing people you actually love is even worse, right? Losing your dad, which you felt you should have been able to control, losing me, which you're sure will eventually happen if you...and we're so important to each other; please know that I know that, and I would never disappear. Not if you let yourself– not if we were...You would never let me down. You couldn't. We'd get through it all together; we'd traverse the endless series of days like explorers in a ship made of time itself, its delicate sails moving easily through the churning water...And your greatest desire? Easy. To be loved, of course. By everyone. Indiscriminately. Unconditionally. But what you don't know is that my love alone would actually be enough. It always has been; it gets you through much more than you give it credit for. If it weren't for me, for instance, this guy wouldn't be here. We both know that.

> *Beat.*

It's you, Sarah. You're you. Do you get it?

SARAH: I get it.

SAM: What's going on?

NATE: I think it's time for the bubbly.

> *He pours it into three glasses, but only he picks his up. He drains the glass and refills it.*

How about a toast.

No one says anything.

No? Then I'll make one myself. I will toast toast. How warming it can be on a cold morning. How, if you don't burn it, it can really hit the spot.

SAM: You're not funny, you know that.

NATE: Oh, I know that.

SAM: *(To SARAH.)* Shouldn't he leave?

SARAH: Nate, can I talk to you?

NATE: I thought you'd never ask.

SARAH: Sam, I'm sorry. Just give us a sec.

SAM: You've gotta be kidding me.

SARAH: Just a second–please.

SAM throws up his hands and exits.

SARAH: What are you doing?

NATE: Drinking.

SARAH: You can't do this.

NATE: Can't do what.

SARAH: Sabotage me.

NATE: That's what you think I'm doing?

SARAH: It's what you're doing. Whether or not you're aware of it.

NATE: I don't think so.

SARAH: You always know exactly what you're doing.

NATE: My life is a real indication of that, isn't it.

SARAH: Just stop this, Nate. Just stop it. Your life is fine.

NATE: No it isn't.

SARAH: What's so awful?

NATE: "When I consider the short duration of my life, swallowed up in an eternity before and after, the little space I fill engulfed in the infinite immensity of spaces whereof I know nothing, and which know nothing of me, I am terrified. The eternal silence of these infinite spaces frightens me."

SARAH: What is that?

NATE: Pascal. I ran it by my kids the other day, and I don't think they fully appreciated it.

SARAH: You didn't.

NATE: I'm scared. Sometimes I think there might be no God.

SARAH: But you've never believed in God.

NATE: I believe in you.

SARAH: You're not making sense.

NATE: And you've abandoned me.

SARAH: That's ridiculous.

NATE: Is it? After all these years. Of waiting.

SARAH: You haven't been waiting for me. This is in your head. This is a new idea, that you've been pining after me all these years. It's not real.

NATE: Come on. Really?? I've never known you to lie, Sarah. Especially not to yourself.

SAM: *(Entering, and across the stage from them.)* What's happening over there? You need me, Sarah?

NATE: Do you need him, Sarah?

> *Beat.*

Do you?

SARAH: *(Quietly but firmly.)* Yes.

NATE: That guy?

SARAH: Nate. Please.

NATE: Please what?

SARAH: I love him.

NATE: But you love me more.

SARAH: *(Quietly.)* You're an asshole, you know that?

NATE: I know that.

SARAH: Well then why don't you stop.

NATE: Remember how in high school we'd be at those parties all night long under the bridge; those nights that went on for fucking-ever, and when the sun started rising, we knew it was finally time to go home and sleep?

SARAH: I remember.

NATE: Well, day isn't starting. I keep waiting for it and it won't start.

SAM: *(Calling out.)* Do you need me?

SARAH: We'll be done in a second!

NATE: Did you hear me? I'm at the edge of something. The real edge.

SARAH: I hear you: you're at the edge. But we can't do this right now. I feel bad.

NATE: You feel bad.

SARAH: Yes.

SAM enters.

SAM: I think I'm gonna go. Okay?

SARAH: What?

SAM: This isn't…I don't mean to be a dick, but I guess I think I should go.

NATE: I appreciate when people acknowledge they can't help being what they are.

SARAH: Nate!

SAM: Yeah. So you can call me if you want.

SARAH: What does that mean?

SAM: I think I'm being pretty clear. I don't live here. I have another place to be. And I'm gonna go be there.

SARAH: No—please don't go.

NATE: We were having such fun.

SAM: *(With dripping sarcasm.)* It was great to meet you, buddy.

SARAH: Sam: stay.

NATE: You can't blame him. He's in over his head. Up against too big a wall. The bulldozer is threatening to crush him. It's getting closer, like a terrible wave. The past rears its ugly head and opens its gigantic salivating maw…

SARAH: It's too much, Nate. You have to stop.

NATE: I can't. Not until you come back with me. Let me take you back.

SARAH: No.

NATE: Come with me for a second. It's almost a year ago. It's winter-time. Brooklyn is as bleak as it's ever been. There's ice on the sidewalks and people slip and fall and break their necks. The cold isn't letting up.

SARAH: What did I just say??

NATE: It's February. You haven't gone to work in three weeks. They're starting to think you might not be coming back. Maybe you're mourning more than just your dad.

SARAH: Stop it. I can see what you're doing and it's not gonna work.

NATE: What am I doing?

SAM: Come on, man. Let's both go. We'll both go.

(He takes his arm, but NATE resists.)

NATE: *(With heat and urgency, nearly frantic.)*

No you want to hear this too. Because I come over here. Sarah is lying on the couch under all these blankets. /I take them off, one by one.

SARAH: I said / stop it.

NATE: I rub her toes and the soles of her feet and her ankles and her calves. I am trying to warm her, to bring her back to life.

SARAH: Don't say another word.

NATE: And then I am lying on top of her on the couch, on this couch right here, and it is sex unlike any other sex I have ever had. It's so beautiful we're crying, aren't we Sarah? Because it was always going to happen; for so long it had just been this idea, this thing in the air that made it hard to breathe.

She doesn't say anything.

See, she's speechless. That's how incredible it was. But we'd been waiting for each other. All these years. So you have to be quiet for awhile; you have to honor it. We lie there for what feels like hours and I kiss her neck and hold her, and she is naked but I have seen her much more naked than this, and she has seen me, and it's not an embarrassing kind of nakedness because she is me and I am her and finally I get her to laugh a little, and finally the laughing turns into something else and we're making love again, only this time it's wild and joyful and funny–even funny–and after it's over she says she thinks she might be okay. Because we just need people to give us the strength to go a few more days until we can find that strength within ourselves, right Sarah? And it was only when I gave her the strength to go into the world that she found you. It was because of me. I am her strength. I am always inside her.

A long beat.

SAM: *(To SARAH, quietly.)* Is this true?

NATE: Of course it's true.

SARAH: *(To NATE.)* Why are you doing this?

NATE: What do you mean?

SARAH: You of all people should…

NATE: Should what.

SARAH: It hasn't even been a year! And it's Christmas.

NATE: He loved you. So much. And so do I.

SARAH: Why, Nate??

NATE: There isn't a why. It just is. And I'm here to get you. To bring you home.

45

SARAH: I am home.

NATE: Not really.

SAM: You are deeply fucked up, man.

NATE: I couldn't agree more.

SAM: I'm just here, having a quiet night with my girlfriend and you crash in here like a tsunami or something.

NATE: *(Singing.)*
Feliz Navidad
Feliz Navidad
Feliz Navidad
Prospero año y felicidad

SAM: Oh god shut up! Just SHUT. UP. I mean, it's all bullshit. Every word you say is some new variation of bullshit!

NATE: You're some new variation of bullshit.

SAM: Fuck you.

NATE: Fuck you.

SARAH: Fuck you both! Just stop it, fucking stop it.

NATE: *(To SAM.)* The thing is: I know you. And you can't stand that.

SAM: Oh, you know me?

SARAH: I'm not gonna listen to this.

SAM: What do you know about me? Tell me.

NATE: It's too easy.

SAM: Fucking tell me then.

NATE: Oh god…Where to start?

SAM: You don't know me.

NATE: You pretend not to care what you look like but you invariably spend fifteen minutes in front of the mirror before you leave the house. You play the guitar because you liked the way guys looked with guitars and then you got some girl because of some song at some point so you kept playing.

SAM: Keep going.

NATE: Okay. In college, you wore the same pair of jeans every day and only read as much of your books as you needed to in order to make one scintillating comment in each class. Your mom says "Oh, Sam" when her friends ask about you: "He'll figure himself out one day." Your parents are more supportive than you deserve given how little time and thought you devote to them.

SAM: Nope, my parents are not supportive.

SARAH: Not everyone coddles their kids / forever, Nate.

NATE: Mostly, your time and thought reside in the dark and drafty residence of one Mademoiselle Envy, and her little ward, schadenfreude, an impish child with acne and clubbed feet. The child you try to suppress but can't, and the former, the Mademoiselle, is everywhere.

SARAH: No, that's YOU. That's you. You're the jealous / one.

NATE: Jealousy of the singer whose songs are like yours but better. Jealousy viewed through the lens of your once huge potential that now, ten years down the line, seems smaller, more improbable, and shifts restlessly in its cage, suddenly desperate as it starts to realize it will never escape, and it can't get out, can it, because if it did and shriveled up, then you'd be truly impotent, even more than you already are, and you already are—trust me—I can tell from the way Sarah looks at you that she doesn't want / you.

SARAH: What are you talking / about?

NATE: She tolerates you. She might even believe she loves you, but it's not an all-consuming love. It's not "we must love one another or die." It's not Auden, and it's not poetry. It's the definition of ho-hum, just like you.

> *Beat. Then SAM punches NATE. It's an awkward punch but it lands and NATE goes down, his nose bleeding; SARAH rushes over.*

SARAH: *(To NATE.)* See? Now look what you've done. Look what you've done.

NATE: What I've done? *(To SAM.)* By the way, I knew you were going to do that. I wanted you to. And you did. As predictable as a peacock.

SARAH leans down and holds a tissue to NATE's nose.

Never hit anyone before, have you? How's it feel?

SAM: He's gotta leave, Sarah. He's gotta leave right now.

NATE: The truth is a fucking drag, isn't it?

SAM: Right now.

SARAH: He's bleeding.

SAM: Now.

NATE: *(Wheedling.)* But I'm in pain.

SAM: No one enjoys rejection, man. You just gotta man up and bear it.

NATE: I haven't been rejected.

SAM: I'd never even heard of you before you came waltzing in here. How do you spin that?

NATE: She didn't tell you about me because she's in love with me. Obviously.

SAM: She's not.

NATE: Well, she's not in love with you.

SARAH: Yes, I am!

NATE: Bullshit.

SAM: You know what it seems like to me?

NATE: Enlighten me.

SAM: *(Slowly.)* It seems like you have this thing where you tell yourself that you understand everyone and everything, but…really it's to make up for your own depths of emptiness and uncertainty. Which I have a feeling are fucking bottomless.

NATE: Oh, they are.

SARAH: Sam, don't–

SAM: *Sam* don't?

NATE: No, you've pegged me, man. I am guilty as charged. You know, I've always wanted to be understood–truly understood–and you've finally done it. So, thank you. I owe you a tremendous debt of gratitude.

SAM: He's gotta go, Sarah. Right now. Or I do.

SARAH: Please…You can't ask that of me. He's my…

>*A breath.*

SAM: He's your what?

SARAH: I just…I can't kick him out.

>*Beat.*

NATE: *(Quietly triumphant.)* I think she made her pick. I think I heard her make her pick.

SARAH: I didn't make a pick. This isn't a game!

NATE: I think I heard you. Or were those just echoes from the future? From a few minutes from now when you kick this guy out and we're alone together, finally.

SARAH: *(Unable to contain it anymore.)* Oh god, I don't want you, Nate, okay?!

>*Beat.*

NATE: What?

SARAH: I said I don't want you.

NATE: But it'll be so nice, Sarah. Finally.

SARAH: You know, Sam asks me about my day and notices little things you'd never notice because at base you're just self-absorbed. Incredibly self-absorbed.

NATE: That's what you want? Someone who's gonna ask you about your day?

SARAH: Yes!

SAM: That's not all I am. Come on, don't bolster his fucking argument!

SARAH: No, you're not. Of course you're not. You're patient and strong and compassionate and your songs make me cry because you are in every note, the sweetest soul I've ever known...And I do think we'll get married one day. I really do. I hope so.

NATE: Are you trying to torture me?

SARAH: You're a child, Nate. That's what you are.

> *Beat.*

NATE: *(Quietly.)* That does seem to be the consensus.

SARAH: What does that mean?

NATE: I was over at my parents' tonight and they were telling me for the zillionth time that they don't understand why I am the way I am; they said it's unusual, and that I just need to accept that things are what they are, and then I'll be content. And I said no thank you—I can't accept that my life disappears behind me like a retreating wave, never to be seen again. I can't accept that. I mean, how can you live that way, with this big hole trailing always behind you?

SARAH: Don't think about things that way. I've told you so many times...

NATE: And I said to them, I said I won't be content, I can't be, until you and I are together, and just as I said it—BAM—I knew it was true. It's the truth and I've always known it but now it was out there, spoken out loud, real and solid like something you can hold in your hands.

SARAH: You said that to them?

NATE: And they said I'm fooling myself. They said there's not one thing that'll solve my...They said Nate, it's just that you've never grown up. That you won't grow up because growing up means acknowledging that life isn't perfect. But for a second, I could tell, they saw it as clearly as I did: the future, and it is perfect—a Sunday morning in spring and they've come to visit. You and my mother stand in the kitchen, drinking tea, while our kids sit on my dad's lap, wanting to be still, to be quiet, but I can't let them. I want to play. I want to swing them in the air like kites, watching

the wind take them into the uppermost reaches of the sky.
I can't get enough, and their little feet and little toes tap the
ground to the beat of my heart. This is the future, and it's
as clear to my parents now as it always has been for me.
So they ask what I'm waiting for. Why not make it happen.
No time like the present, right? So I hightail it over here,
and I've never gotten somewhere so quickly, never been
so sure.

I'm in love with you, Louise. And we can be our parents.
We can have children; we can grow up.

> *SARAH turns to the audience, but the emotion of the moment
> doesn't break.*

SARAH: Years from now, I still replay it. I'll be walking down
the street, alone or with my children, even with them, and
it will hit me with a whoosh like something pressing up
against my…something pressing up against my heart my
chest my spleen has suddenly been released and it takes
me over so that I can barely stand. What I could have
done, who I might have been. I hear all of the different
futures inside of me, singing. My knees buckle. I feel like I
can't breathe. That is the effect it has. It still has.

NATE: I know you love me too. I know it.

SARAH: Of course I love you too. Sometimes it hurts my heart
how much I love you.

NATE: So then what are we waiting for? We don't have to wait
anymore.

SARAH: Nate.

NATE: Sarah.

SARAH: I just…it's overwhelming. It's too much.

NATE: But not too much for you.

SARAH: Yes, for me.

NATE: Please don't.

> *Beat.*

You can save me. Please save me.

SARAH: Save you from what? What can I give you? It's a delusion. There is no perfect life like the one you imagine. I mean, my parents were practically divorced before he died.

NATE: That's not true.

SARAH: It is true. It might've been what killed him. And when he died –

SAM: Okay, you don't have to–Sarah, you don't have to talk about it.

SARAH: You didn't see it…The way the body knows right away…It changes color–did you know that? It is the definition of loneliness. Of being abandoned…No. None of us can be saved. That's the emptiness at the heart of…That is the emptiness.

And that is where you live. Surrounded by all that emptiness.

NATE: I wouldn't if I was with you.

SARAH: I don't know. I don't know that. And I can't live my life feeling like everything good is behind me…And I actually don't think you really know me if you can't see that.

So. Please. Please, Nate. Let me go.

Beat.

NATE: You're cruel, do you know that?

SARAH: I'm sorry.

NATE: You're a fucking bitch, do you know that?

SAM: Okay–

SARAH: I'm so sorry–

NATE: No, you are. And you always have been.

SAM: Nope, we won't have any of that.

SAM starts to usher NATE to the door.

NATE: Do you know what I would do for you? What I would have done for you? You will never in your life be loved in the way I loved you...And, you know, I'm glad your fucking father died. Serves you right. You deserve to be alone.

SAM: That's it. That's enough.

SAM pushes NATE over the threshold of the door.

NATE: Enough of what?

SAM: We've had enough of you for now, okay? Let it be. Go home.

NATE: I am home.

SARAH: Go, Nate.

NATE: You said you wouldn't kick me out.

SARAH: I know.

NATE: I'm sorry I said that about your father. I didn't mean it.

SARAH: I know.

NATE: Do I really have to go?

SARAH: You really do.

> *Beat.*

Go...Go, Nate.

> *NATE looks at her hard. They stare into and through each other. Then NATE leaves. A long silence. SAM and SARAH don't look at each other. And then they do. SAM goes to her and holds her. They stand still; SARAH is crying. She whispers.*

I'm sorry.

SAM: I know.

> *A song. They kiss, very tenderly, lovingly.*

SAM: And then we looked out the window. At the skyline across the water, the Christmas lights of the Empire State Building. The stars.

SARAH: There weren't any stars.

SAM: No?

SARAH: What if we just hadn't opened the door?

SAM: He knocked. It was Christmas Eve.

SARAH: It was a starless night. And time…time zig-zagged across the sky, back and forth and back and forth. Time was moving in a new way. Different than it ever had before.

SAM: It never ends.

SARAH: The night never ends. Because if it ends.

SAM: It doesn't end.

SARAH: And yet. This was years ago.

SAM: At a certain point in life, everything is years ago.

SARAH: The poem Nate brought me was Auden's "Musée Des Beaux Arts."

SAM: *(To the audience.)* Sarah and I only saw each other once more after that night.

SARAH: A poem about Breugel's painting "Landscape with the Fall of Icarus." Of course Breugel.

SAM: A poem based on a painting, a painting curled into a poem. I'd read it in school.

SARAH: It's about what happens when no one is watching.

SAM: And how the world moves on.

SARAH: You have to look at the painting carefully before you discover what it's about. At first it looks like nothing is wrong. A man and a wagon go down a hill. There's the ocean, and a ship. A clear blue sky.

SAM: The world outside the window seemed quiet, peaceful even.

SARAH: Then you notice that in the corner a boy is falling into the sea, falling from the sky into the sea, his legs up in the air, the rest of him already submerged. He is disappearing as we watch.

> *She reads from the poem.*

About suffering they were never wrong,
The old Masters: how well they understood

Its human position: how it takes place
While someone else is eating or opening a window or just
walking dully along…

SAM: We were looking out the window.

SARAH: A light came pouring in. A red moving light. Like
someone's heart revolving.

SAM: One day, my son will ask me how our hearts work,
how our bodies keep us alive. And I will flash back to
that beating red light, moving in its orbit, like an obedient
planet.

SARAH: It was only later, home from college, that I realized
the Tower of Babel was crumbling. It wasn't idyllic at all.
Our imaginary place.

SAM: We opened the window and the cold air came rushing in.

SARAH: My mother once asked me if there was anything
between me and Nate. "Me and Nate?" I laughed. No.
There's nothing there. Me and Nate. I couldn't get over it.
She looked at me strangely. Methinks the lady doth protest
too much. My mother said.

SAM: Should we go down there?

SARAH: It's freezing out.

SAM: They've been down there a long time. I can't see what's
going on.

SARAH: You can go down if you want.

SAM: Yeah?

SARAH: *(Joking.)* As long as you promise you'll come back.

SAM: I promise.

> *He throws on a jacket and exits. Across the stage, a light*
> *illuminates NATE.*

NATE: I don't think about the world. The beautiful world.
Until later. First it's Sarah looking at me from across the
room in a crowded party. Somehow I am always in high
school, in a crowded room that smells of pot and sweat,
and the music is too loud, and she can't hear me. Was

there a time when I was happy? If there was, this was it, this moment when I was starting to figure out my own power, and believe in the vast promise that was me. And this woman—not really a girl anymore—across the room. Looking at me.

And then it gets very quiet. And there's the sensation of being outside of myself, a boy watching another boy, and he doesn't want to stop him, and he doesn't want to interfere. And now we're somewhere else: the meadow near the cottage in Maine that my parents sometimes rented in August when it got too hot in the city.

The sun is setting and the boy walks over to the lone tree in the middle of the vast meadow. He's as alone as he's ever been, under that tree, its branches the expanse of time itself, how everything was here before him and will be here after he's gone. And full of impossible beauty.

And it's at this point that the boy watching tries to speak: "stop," he tries to say, "stop. You could still make something beautiful, something lasting," but he can't make even a sound, and he can't move. He's enveloped in this strange, warm embrace and the grass sways and the breeze makes the leaves flutter… and he sleeps.

> *SAM returns. He opens the door slowly and closes it behind him carefully, slowly.*

SARAH: What was it?

SAM: I can't…

SARAH: You can't what?

SAM: Sarah.

SARAH: What?

SAM: I wanted to say: let's go out the back door. Let's escape.

SARAH: What is it?

SAM: I can't.

SARAH: Sam??

SAM: I can't be the one to…

SARAH: What? What happened?

SAM: Icarus, I wanted to say.

SARAH: Tell me, Sam. You have to tell me, Sam.

SAM: And she was shaking me and I was frightened and I didn't know what to do so I told her.

> *Beat.*

SARAH: He what?

> *Quietly.*

He did what?

SAM: I don't know how to–

SARAH: He did what?

SAM: I don't–

SARAH: That's not possible.

SAM: I know, I–

SARAH: It's someone else.

SAM: Sarah.

SARAH: What happened? Tell me again.

SAM: I guess they think he…jumped. I guess that's what they think.

SARAH: What? Where was he? He jumped from where?

SAM: I told you.

SARAH: Tell me again.

SAM: *(To the audience.)* And so I told her again.

SARAH: No. It's not actually him.

SAM: We were stuck in a loop.

SARAH: Time was zig-zagging across the sky. It was earlier that night, it was earlier that week, it was the rest of our lives, all at once.

SAM: I was Derek Jeter. Not so long ago, I was Derek Jeter. And that was kinda funny because I'm a Mets fan. Not so long ago I was Samuel Robert Hirsch—that's how they said it at my high school graduation, the whole thing, drawn out, each syllable, as though you've suddenly really earned your name. And now I'm…Well I guess I'm still that person, but it feels like something like this should change your name. It feels like you should wear it like a badge over your…Like a sign on your forehead.

SARAH: The ease of childhood, maybe, the being taken care of, the attention, the way you're amazing if you manage to both wash your face and brush your teeth. My mother said Nate's parents idolized him. Made him feel he was superior to everyone and everything so inevitably the whole world felt disappointing. A little bit grey.

SAM: In the future, I write songs around it. And then, finally, once I am well known enough to do the things I want to do, I make an album called Nate and Sarah. And the song I am most proud of is called "Love Song to Our Parents."

SARAH: In the future, I'm more careful. Like a woman always about to trip. In the future, I watch people closely.

SAM: The future. What does that even mean? And yet, it happens. Suddenly you're in it, whether you like it or not. Mine includes a late Sunday afternoon in Prospect Park. New Year's Day of a year that at some point in my childhood would have seemed unbelievable. Incredible to think I'd ever live in that particular year, because it would mean I'd be older than my parents, older than my 2nd grade teacher. Forty-five. Some number like forty-five.

SARAH: We're both out running in Prospect Park.

SAM: It's been over ten years but she looks the same. Frozen in time…Sarah! I call out to her. Sarah!

SARAH: I slow down. I know that voice.

SAM: Sarah.

SARAH: Hey, I say.

SAM: Hey.

SARAH: Wow.

SAM: Sam Hirsch.

SARAH: I know who you are.

SAM: I figured, I just…Well, you never know, right?

SARAH: And it's one of those moments where the whoosh takes over and I have to sit down on the grass.

SAM sits next to her.

SAM: Are you okay?

SARAH: I think so. I just got a little…light-headed. I'm okay.

SAM: How are you? – Is that the right thing to ask?

SARAH: I guess so?

SAM: Well, good, I…

SARAH: I've heard some of your music, you know.

SAM: Yeah?

SARAH: It's good. It's still really good.

SAM: Thanks…It's been a trip.

SARAH: What?

SAM: Oh just the band and…you know I never expected it.

SARAH: I know, but I did.

Awkward beat.

SAM: So are you still at that agency? The old people and…

SARAH: Oh–no. I went to law school.

SAM: You went to…

SARAH: I'm a lawyer.

SAM: Do you like it?

SARAH: I don't know.

SAM: Sorry–was that a lame…?

SARAH: No…No. It's just…

SAM: Are you married?

SARAH: Two kids and everything.

SAM: Wow.

SARAH: Your wife is very beautiful...

SAM: Careful, you'll make me blush.

SARAH: She is.

SAM: Who's your—I mean...

SARAH: We met in law school.

SAM: Where was that?

SARAH: California.

SAM: Wow, you got far away.

SARAH: I got far away.

SAM: What brought you back?

SARAH: Home, I guess...

> *Beat.*

I wanted my kids to know my mom.

SAM: That must be nice. To be close to her.

SARAH: Yeah, it was...She passed away last year, so.

SAM: Oh, I'm sorry.

SARAH: No, it's...I mean, yeah...But it sort of releases you too. You know?

SAM: Yeah.

SARAH: I don't mean to be...But yeah.

SAM: You can be...I don't mind.

SARAH: Are you happy, Sam?

SAM: What?

SARAH: Are you happy?

SAM: I don't know how to answer that question.

SARAH: I think your songs are kind of sad. They used to be...I don't know. More upbeat.

SAM: Time's passed, you know? It keeps going.

SARAH: I love being a mother. I didn't think I would. I didn't want children. I thought I'd be too afraid of everything.

SAM: I remember.

SARAH: We talked about that?

SAM: Sarah.

SARAH: It's seriously all such a blur.

SAM: I thought I would marry you. I was sure I'd marry you.

SARAH: I know...

> *They look at each other.*

And it's strange.

SAM: What is?

SARAH: How can I have children I said to David–that's my husband. I am a child. I can't have children. I am a child.

SAM: And?

SARAH: You have them anyway...And then you grow up.

> *The lights slowly fade.*

BOY

Characters

DR. WENDELL BARNES

40s-50s, warm and genial. He's passionate about his work and his ideals; he's the smartest guy in the room but tries hard not to show it

ADAM TURNER

early-mid 20s, working class but self-educated, gentle, raw

JENNY LAFFERTY

Adam's girlfriend (early-mid 20s), Jenny is a bit toughened and wary but still hoping for wonderful things, working class

TRUDY TURNER

Adam's mother (30s-40s); warm and lost and hopeful, trying to make sense of a confusing world and doing her best

DOUG TURNER

Adam's father (30s-40s), a man of not very many words, working class and in over his head, just trying to get by

Setting
Davenport, Iowa and Boston, Massachusetts

Time
The play spans many years—from 1968-1990

Note
This play is a work of fiction, though it is inspired by a true story.

Boy was originally produced by the Keen Company in a co-production with the Ensemble Studio Theatre and the Alfred P. Sloan Foundation (Keen Company's Artistic Director is Jonathan Silverstein; Ensemble Studio Theatre's Artistic Director is William Carden) on February 23, 2016. The director was Linsay Firman, the stage manager Rhonda Picou, the set designer Sandra Goldmark, the lighting designer Nick Francone, the sound designer Shane Rettig and the costume designer Sydney Maresca. The cast was as follows:

DR. WENDELL BARNES	Paul Niebanck
ADAM TURNER	Bobby Steggert
JENNY LAFFERTY	Rebecca Rittenhouse
TRUDY TURNER	Heidi Armbruster
DOUG TURNER	Ted Koch

They fuck you up, your mum and dad.
  They may not mean to, but they do.
They fill you with the faults they had
  And add some extra, just for you.

But they were fucked up in their turn
  By fools in old-style hats and coats,
Who half the time were soppy-stern
  And half at one another's throats.

Man hands on misery to man.
  It deepens like a coastal shelf.
Get out as early as you can,
  And don't have any kids yourself.

Philip Larkin, *This Be the Verse*

Learn from me, if not by my precepts, at least by my example, how dangerous is the achievement of knowledge, and how much happier that man is who believes his native town to be the world, than he who aspires to become greater than his nature will allow.

Mary Shelley, *Frankenstein*

There is no surer way to screw up an experiment than to be certain of its outcome.

Stuart Firestein, *Ignorance: How it Drives Science*

Neither in environment nor in heredity can I find the exact instrument that fashioned me, the anonymous roller that pressed upon my life a certain intricate watermark…

Vladimir Nabokov, *Speak, Memory*

Did I request thee, Maker, from my clay
To mould me Man? Did I solicit thee
From darkness to promote me?

John Milton, *Paradise Lost*

…but Max stepped into his private boat and waved goodbye
and sailed back over a year
and in and out of weeks
and through a day
and into the night of his very own room

Maurice Sendak, *Where the Wild Things Are*

Darkness. Then against the darkness, a Projection: 1989. Halloween. And then the lights slam on, hard; a door opens and with it come the loud sounds of a party – music, yelling. ADAM and JENNY fly through the door and slam it shut, at which point the noise stops as abruptly as it began. ADAM is dressed as Frankenstein's monster and Jenny as a bunny. ADAM wears a half-mask over his eyes.

ADAM and JENNY are breathless and talk too loud because they can't hear each other—their ears are still ringing.

JENNY: Oh my lord!

ADAM: I know!

JENNY: I'm so sorry! Cindy…usually she's got better music…I mean, usually it's not so loud!

ADAM: *(Still shouting.)* Hey, do you recognize me?

JENNY: What??

ADAM: I know you! Do you know me?

JENNY: Can *you* hear anything?

ADAM: I can hear you.

JENNY: I can see your mouth moving but oh my gosh, I can't hear you. This is so weird!

ADAM: You still look the same.

JENNY: What?

ADAM: Wanna sit?

JENNY: *(She hasn't heard him; she still speaks very loud.)* I think I'm just gonna sit down!

ADAM: Great!

> *They sit.*

So you really don't, um –

JENNY: If I can't hear you, I guess we can't really talk.

> *She does something flirtatious, putting her hand on ADAM's leg, or arm. ADAM's longing is heartbreakingly clear, but he moves away from her.*

ADAM: *(Really loud.)* You know you probably shouldn't dress like that.

JENNY: What?

ADAM: *(Then louder.)* I said—you really shouldn't dress that way.

JENNY: No I can hear you now. You don't have to shout.

ADAM: Okay.

JENNY: It's just that it's Halloween. Everyone's dressed like something.

ADAM: Here, let me just…

> *He takes off his jacket and drapes it over her shoulders.*

JENNY: *(Weirded out.)* Really?

ADAM: If you don't mind.

JENNY: Well, what are you supposed to be? Frankenstein?

ADAM: Frankenstein was the guy who made the monster. I'm just the monster.

JENNY: If you say so.

ADAM: I wouldn't want to be Frankenstein.

JENNY: Doesn't matter. It's a good costume.

ADAM: It is?

JENNY: I always wear this. I've been the same thing since the tenth grade.

> *She removes the jacket.*

Sorry, but it's kinda warm in here.

ADAM: *(Pretending he doesn't know.)* It's Jenny, right?

JENNY: Did I tell you that?

ADAM: You must have.

JENNY: Or Jen. Jen or Jenny. Doesn't really matter.

ADAM: Well, which do you…

JENNY: In high school there was this teacher Mr. Giannopoulos; he was such a dick, he started calling me Jen even though I corrected him so many times, and then suddenly everyone was calling me Jen. It just stuck.

ADAM: You could un-stick it.

JENNY: That's actually pretty hard. People start thinking about you in a certain way maybe.

ADAM: I don't know. You seem like a Jenny to me.

JENNY: Yeah?

ADAM: When I saw you, I thought, I bet that's Jenny.

JENNY: *(Smiling.)* You didn't.

ADAM: I did.

JENNY: Where are you from again?

ADAM: Oh. Um…Estherville.

JENNY: Shut up!

ADAM: *(Not understanding.)* Okay…

JENNY: No, I mean…why don't I know you?

ADAM: I don't know.

JENNY: We used to go to Estherville all the time. I went to school there. I grew up in Spirit Lake. You know Spirit Lake, right?

ADAM: Yeah, I–

JENNY: You probably never even went it's so tiny. Where'd you go to school?

ADAM: Oh, just this small…Catholic school. Outside the city.

JENNY: I was so happy to get away from there, weren't you? When Cindy told me about this job, I didn't think; I just left. Drove halfway across the state. She found me this shithole of an apartment next to hers–

ADAM: *(Hiding his interest.)* You live next-door?

JENNY: Yeah I think my bedroom is on the other side of this wall.

Laughing to herself.

Good thing you can't see into it; it's a fucking disaster.

ADAM: I bet it's great.

JENNY: *(Matter-of-fact.)* No it sucks. And the job *really* sucks. At Quick-Rite. There's this Trekkie kid Eric who's sixteen but we have the exact same job. It's like…embarrassing. And all day long, it's Captain Spock this, Captain Spock that. I can't stand it.

ADAM: Captain Kirk. Spock is a first officer.

JENNY: Excuse me?

ADAM: Nothing.

JENNY: And Cindy took off after I was there two weeks. I guess she thought there were better jobs out there or something.

ADAM: *(A bit too aggressively.)* Cindy is such a bitch. I hate her.

JENNY: …Whoa…I was joking, ok? There *are* better jobs out there. Basically any job…

Just lighten up, mister monster. You are a strange one, aren't you.

ADAM: *(Really asking.)* Am I strange?

JENNY: *(Take what I say with a grain of salt.)*

I'm drunk.

ADAM: Yeah there's just…can I just…you've got a little foam kinda over your lip–

He reaches towards her face but doesn't actually touch her.

JENNY: Oh!

JENNY wipes it off.

ADAM: Sorry, that was–it was sort of like a little mustache.

JENNY: Oh God! You thought I had a mustache?

ADAM: Like Charlie Chaplin.

JENNY: Who's that?

ADAM: Charlie Chaplin?

JENNY: I'm awful; I don't know any current pop anything. Ask me anything and I won't know it.

ADAM: Well, it's not so current.

JENNY: *(Suddenly remembering.)* Hey! Cindy told me you know a lot about cars.

ADAM: Yeah, I–

JENNY: Well, God bless you. I hate my car. It craps out on me all the time.

ADAM: What kind of car?

JENNY: '82 Honda Accord.

ADAM: That's pretty nice–front wheel drive, four cylinder engine, four-wheel independent suspension–that's a good car.

JENNY: I don't know any of that, but sure.

ADAM: How does it crap out on you?

JENNY: Like the battery dies a lot. Just stops dead.

ADAM: You must not be turning off your dome light.

JENNY: My dome light?

ADAM: Yeah–the light above the dash. You might think it goes off automatically, but this one doesn't. You have to turn it off manually. Otherwise, it drains the battery like crazy.

JENNY: Really?

ADAM: Really.

JENNY: Gosh, that might be it.

ADAM: That's definitely it.

JENNY: How'd you get to know so much about cars?

ADAM: I guess I sort of taught myself.

JENNY: *(Flirty.)* So as a little boy you were always under the family car, that kinda thing?

ADAM: I don't know. I think if you love something enough you can pretty much learn it.

> *Breath. She takes this in. He gazes at her, then puts his hand on her leg.*

You can teach yourself almost anything, I think.

JENNY: You really think that?

ADAM: Yeah.

> *She really looks at him.*

JENNY: You wanna teach *me* about cars?

ADAM: Oh—um, sure—

JENNY: I'd go under a car with you, I think.

ADAM: What?

JENNY: You could take me under a car with you. I'd go.

> *Beat. She takes off Adam's mask, and then whispers.*

You wanna kiss me, Adam?

ADAM: Yeah.

> *She leans in but he doesn't move.*

JENNY: You can then, if you want to.

> *He doesn't move.*

JENNY: *(Recoiling, hurt.)* I mean, you don't have to.

ADAM: *(Quietly.)* No, I want to.

> *Then, from across the stage.*

WENDELL: *(Warmly.)* Samantha, can you come and sit down now?

ADAM: *(To JENNY.)* I want to.

> *He crosses into the scene with Wendell, where he now enacts SAMANTHA, his younger self. A Projection: 1973. SAMANTHA is 6.*
>
> *A tape recorder is whirring.*

WENDELL: All right! Let's have you sitting up straight. Yes—
that's good. Oh—remember to cross your legs—like this.

She obliges.

Good. Now for the benefit of the recording, I'm just going
to say: this is our first visit of Samantha's first grade year.

SAMANTHA: Last year I was in kindergarten.

WENDELL: That's absolutely right.

SAMANTHA: You said I was your favorite kindergartner.

WENDELL: And now you're my favorite first grader.
Tell me: how are you liking it so far?

SAMANTHA: It's okay.

WENDELL: Are most of your friends at school boys or girls?

SAMANTHA: Girls.

WENDELL writes something on a clipboard.

WENDELL: Good. And what do you like to do with them? In
your free time, when you play.

SAMANTHA: Dolls.

WENDELL: And what do you enact with the dolls? What
stories do you tell?

SAMANTHA: I don't know.

WENDELL: Family stories? Stories where a mother and a father
take care of and play with and raise their children?

SAMANTHA: Yes!

WENDELL: Good. Good! And does your brother play with
dolls with you?

SAMANTHA: Once we put some dolls in his garbage truck and
churned them all into shreds.

WENDELL: In your imagination, you mean?

SAMANTHA: But then my mom told me "no playing with the
truck. That's boy stuff."

WENDELL: Did she. And was that okay by you?

SAMANTHA: Well, we made cookies instead. But I didn't like them; they had raisins.

WENDELL: What are you working on in school right now?

SAMANTHA: I had to do a report on whales.

WENDELL: Oh, I love whales! What kind of whales?

SAMANTHA: Humpback.

WENDELL: Humpback whales. Very nice.

SAMANTHA: I wanted to do it on bugs but Mrs. Barber said no.

WENDELL: Well, bugs are a little icky, are they not? A little gross?

SAMANTHA: I don't think bugs are gross.

WENDELL: Why did Mrs. Barber say you couldn't write your report on bugs?

SAMANTHA: Because everyone had to write about whales, which wasn't fair.

WENDELL laughs.

WENDELL: You know, sometimes we have to do things we don't really want to do, Samantha. And those things might even be good for us.

SAMANTHA: Why is it good for me to know about whales?

WENDELL: It's good to learn about the world in general. To find out what's in it. What's out there.

SAMANTHA: I know what's in it.

WENDELL: And what's that?

SAMANTHA: People. Cars. Trees. Bugs. Iowa, which is a state in the United States where I live. And cartoons, thank goodness.

WENDELL: Thank goodness.

SAMANTHA: And Budweiser.

WENDELL: Excuse me?

SAMANTHA: Budweiser. It's a kind of beer.

WENDELL writes something on the clipboard.

WENDELL: Samantha…Does your father drink a lot of Budweiser?

SAMANTHA: You drink a lot of coffee.

WENDELL: I do. I drink a lot of coffee.

SAMANTHA: My dad says coffee tastes like ass.

WENDELL: That's not a very nice thing to say.

SAMANTHA: Not nice things to say are in the world.

WENDELL: Well, yes, that's true, but–

SAMANTHA: Also Pizza. Stephen. Dresses.

WENDELL: You're wearing a lovely one today.

SAMANTHA: You like it?

WENDELL: I love it.

SAMANTHA: Oh. Good.

WENDELL: You really are a remarkable child, do you know that?

SAMANTHA: No I'm not.

WENDELL: You are.

SAMANTHA: *(Unable to repress a smile.)* Like, more than Stephen?

WENDELL: Well, I'm sure Stephen is quite wonderful–

SAMANTHA: No, he's not.

WENDELL: Either way, you are my primary interest.

SAMANTHA: *(Proudly.)* I am your primary interest.

WENDELL: Do you know what primary means?

SAMANTHA shakes her head.

It means number one. So you are my number one interest. You are number one in my book, okay Samantha?

A hesitation, and then…

SAMANTHA: Okay.

The lights shift.

A Projection: 1968.

DOUG and TRUDY write a letter. WENDELL listens.

TRUDY: Dear Dr. Wendell Barnes:

Last night I saw you speak on *60 Minutes* with Mike Wallace. You were very dignified! And my but you've written so many books! Also, I liked that you didn't rise to the bait when Wallace asked how it felt to play God. I think maybe some people have to play God every now and then. I mean, I think you're a real hero. The way you've helped all those people. Regular folks who don't feel like what they are so you just change them. You take them seriously when no one else will.

Struggling with and mispronouncing the word.

And the herm...herma...phro...

DOUG: Hermaphrodites.

TRUDY: I know how to say it, Doug.

DOUG: Okay.

TRUDY: You help them too. And they turn out okay whether they're brought up as boys or girls. Which I think is just so so interesting.

DOUG: *(Prompting her to get back on track.)* Anyway. We're writing because...

TRUDY: Yes, because we have identical twin boys, Stephen and Samuel. They're nearly one now. Our son, Sam, had an accident when he was eight months old. We were told to circumcise the boys, owing to the phimosis, and when the doctor went first to circumcise Sam, the cautery machine didn't work right and ended up destroying the entirety of his, well, his...

DOUG: Penis...Seared it clean off so there's nothing left.

TRUDY: *(With a bitter laugh.)* Of course the doctor didn't go on and do Stephen, and wouldn't you know it but the phimosis went away on its own soon enough.

DOUG: And now we've been all over. And the doctors…they say we're fucked.

TRUDY: Doug!

DOUG: Sam will never lead a normal life. He will never be a father. He will never be normal.

TRUDY: And then we saw you on that program and you said that we are blank slates at birth. You said we are shaped by society and not biology. And you had that lady on with you—well that man who's now a lady and who seems really content with her life, and for the first time in a long time I felt some…hope.

DOUG: We can't go on this way.

My wife is…she won't get out of bed.

TRUDY: That doesn't matter.

DOUG: It matters to me.

TRUDY: Please, doctor.

We love our boy so much.

And he's just a baby.

DOUG: Thanks for your time, doc.
Yours sincerely –

TRUDY: Doug and Trudy Turner.

WENDELL responds. TRUDY and DOUG listen.

WENDELL: Dear Mr. and Mrs. Turner:
Let me say first: never have I encountered a more agonizing story. I'm so very sorry. But I'm glad you found me because together I think we might find a way forward. There are no guarantees in life but there are choices. And right now you're faced with the choice to do nothing or the choice to act, to take a bold risk in the name of easing a young child's burden. Penile reconstruction isn't advanced, so the option remaining to you is to raise your son as a female. To let her live as a whole person as opposed to an incomplete boy, which could well do irreparable damage to the psyche. It's a choice both radical and scary, with

81

a long road ahead—a surgery now to begin construction
of the vagina, hormone treatments, a final surgery down
the line. And perhaps most difficult of all...you could
never tell her. If she knew she was born a boy, that would
complicate the picture too much. You'd have to follow
some guidelines very closely—what to say to her, what not
to say. I'd also monitor her closely—but don't worry, the
hospital would cover all your costs—this would constitute
a very important study. No, none of it would be easy, but,
speaking as a former boy who himself didn't quite fit in,
it seems to me one should do whatever one can to ease
unnecessary suffering, however radical. There is nothing
that brings me greater satisfaction than seeing people
happy who might not have been otherwise—especially
children. And I think, I really do, that if we work together,
if we work as a team, you could have what you're hoping
for: a happy, healthy child.

> *The lights shift.*
>
> *A Projection: 1989.*
>
> *ADAM's at a payphone and calls JENNY at the supermarket
> where she's a cashier. ADAM'S mood has swung up and he's
> on a real high. On the loudspeaker: "Jen Lafferty—phone
> call. Jen Lafferty, you have a phone call." Embarrassed, she
> leaves her post and goes to the phone.)*

JENNY: Hello?

ADAM: Come out with me.

JENNY: Who is this?

ADAM: It's Adam.

JENNY: Adam?

ADAM: From the party last night.

JENNY: *(This is weird.)* Oh. Adam.

ADAM: I wondered if you would come out with me. Like...I
don't know. Like...a date.

JENNY: A date?

ADAM: Yeah. Like, right now.

JENNY: But I'm working.

ADAM: Play hooky. Say you're not feeling well.

JENNY: I can't do that.

ADAM: I want to see you.

JENNY: Well, I get off in a couple hours–

ADAM: It would be great if it could be now.

JENNY: Why?

ADAM: I started worrying I forgot what you looked like.

JENNY: You've gotta be kidding me.

ADAM: Look…I'd be really honored if you came out with me right now, okay? I'd be *honored.* Jenny.

JENNY: Oh Jesus God.

ADAM: What?

JENNY: *(Quietly.)* Okay I'll come.

> *(Even quieter.)*

I'll tell them I'm a little sick.

ADAM: Tell them and then come outside.

JENNY: You're already here?

ADAM: I'm here.

> *The lights shift. She goes outside; they stand in the parking lot together. Now that they're face-to-face, ADAM is a bit shyer.*

ADAM: Hey.

JENNY: Hey.

ADAM: You look beautiful.

JENNY: Oh yeah I really spruced up for the register today.

ADAM: Well, I think you look beautiful.

JENNY: Well…
Thanks.

> *Beat.*

ADAM: So…wanna go for a drive? Or I could look at your car. See if I can't get to the bottom of the battery problem.

JENNY: Did I talk about that?

ADAM: Yeah. A lot.

JENNY: Shit. I really *was* drunk.

ADAM: No, you were fine. You were great.

JENNY: But…I, um…I shouldn't have given the impression I was looking for anything, if that's what I did…Cuz I'm not.

ADAM: Okay.

JENNY: I mean, maybe you already know…

ADAM: Know what?

JENNY: I have a kid.

ADAM: Oh…you have a kid?

JENNY: He's four. Brian.

ADAM: *(Who's the father?)* So –

JENNY: There's no dad. I mean, no dad in the picture…It's so fucking cliché it embarrasses me, but there you go; that's my life.

> *Beat.*

ADAM: So what do you read to him?

JENNY: What?

ADAM: What do you read to your son?

JENNY: *(Surprised.)* Oh…I don't know…

He goes to school in LeClaire, which means I spend all my time driving back and forth. And I guess I mentioned that I hate my car.

ADAM: You did.

JENNY: So yeah, we don't read all that much…

> *Half joking.*

I guess I'm a horrible mother.

ADAM: No, it's just…when I was a kid, all I did was read…I'd spend weeks just reading. Whole summers just reading.

JENNY: *(Teasing.)* Wow, so you were a nerd, huh?

ADAM: No, I was just…sad.

JENNY: *(Surprised and gentle.)* Oh.

ADAM: But, you know…I loved sci-fi, fantasy. *Childhood's End.* Narnia. *Lord of the Rings.* War stuff. Anything to do with war, really. *Catch-22.* I was wrecked by that movie *Bridge On the River Kwai.*

JENNY: That's with Tom Cruise!

ADAM: No.

JENNY: I don't know. We watch a lot of cartoons in my house. Sometimes I don't even notice I'm talking like Elmer Fudd.

ADAM: Do it.

JENNY: No way.

ADAM: Come on, you have to.

JENNY: Oh god…um… *(As ELMER.)* Well…What a wascally wascally wabbit you are.

ADAM: Shh…Be vewwy, vewwy quiet…I'm hunting wabbits!

JENNY: *(Laughing.)* What are we, five years old?

ADAM: I bet you're *such* a good mother, Jenny.

JENNY: *(Genuinely.)* I wish I was.

ADAM: If you brought Brian by the library, I could find him some books. Ones he'd like. I'm there every day.

> *Off her look.*

I mean, I work there. I shelve books.

Anyway, you should come by.

JENNY: *(This probably won't happen.)* Yeah. Maybe.

ADAM: Or if you wanted, I could drive him to school some mornings.

> *She stares at him.*

JENNY: Why would you do that?

ADAM: I don't know. I like driving. And you don't.

JENNY: But you don't know me.

> *Beat.*

ADAM: I feel like I do, though.

JENNY: I can't let you drive my kid to school.

ADAM: Or we could do it together.

> *Beat.*

JENNY: Yeah…so like I said I'm not looking for anything.
…I'm sorry…

ADAM: No—that's okay…

So…

> *Sadly.*

Okay.

> *He's not sure what to do, if he's supposed to stay or walk away. The lights shift.*
>
> *A Projection: 1974. SAMANTHA is 7.*
>
> *SAMANTHA is studying things framed on WENDELL's office walls.*

SAMANTHA: What's that one?

WENDELL: That's my college diploma.

SAMANTHA: It's not in English.

WENDELL: No, it's not.

SAMANTHA: Did you go to a college that wasn't in English?

WENDELL: Some college's diplomas are in Latin because they're old schools, rooted in classical traditions.

> *Onto the next frame.*

SAMANTHA: What's this thing?

WENDELL: It's a poem.

SAMANTHA: Why do you have a poem on your wall?

WENDELL: Because I like it.

SAMANTHA: What's it about?

WENDELL: Why don't you read it and tell me yourself.

SAMANTHA: I hate reading.

WENDELL: No, you don't.

SAMANTHA: Yeah, I do.

WENDELL: Well, it's a simple poem. You'll like it. I came upon it a long time ago, and it's stayed with me all these years.

SAMANTHA: Yeah because it's on your wall.

WENDELL: No I *put* it on my wall because I couldn't forget about it.

SAMANTHA: Why couldn't you?

WENDELL: It's sometimes hard to know why a piece of art speaks to you.

SAMANTHA: Art speaks to you?

WENDELL: Not literally, of course. But art can inspire you. It can move you. I find it humbling that someone as accomplished in his lifetime as Leigh Hunt could be remembered solely for a little poem, sweet as it may be. We have so little control over our legacy. Unless we're Milton, I suppose. Unless we do something astonishing.

SAMANTHA: What's Milton?

WENDELL laughs.

WENDELL: John Milton's a who not a what and just so happens to have authored the finest poem ever written. One day you'll read it and it'll change your life. At the moment, though, I'd like you to read this one to me.

SAMANTHA: No.

WENDELL: Oh come on, I haven't heard it in so long.

SAMANTHA is silent.

It's short! Come on.

SAMANTHA: *(Reading quickly and ignoring line breaks; when mistakes are made, Wendell jumps in with corrections.)*

Jenny kissed me when we met,
Jumping from the chair she sat in.
Time, you thief! who love to get
Sweets into your list, put that in.
Say I'm w[e]ary

WENDELL: Weary. It's pronounced weary.

SAMANTHA: *Say I'm weary, say I'm sad;*
Say that health and wealth have missed me;
Say I'm growing old, but add-
Jenny kissed me!

WENDELL: You did it.

SAMANTHA: You made me.

WENDELL: Did you like the poem?

SAMANTHA: No.

WENDELL: What would you say it was about?

SAMANTHA: Nothing. It was dumb.

WENDELL: *I'd* say it's about how your life is your own. You can miss out on things like health and wealth but you can still find happiness if you look for it. It's all up to you. You tell your own story.

SAMANTHA: *I'd* say it was dumb.

WENDELL: Well, I'm not sure you really heard it; you were too busy sounding out the words.

SAMANTHA: That's not true.

WENDELL: Do you really hate reading, Samantha?

SAMANTHA: *(Looking down in shame.)* I'm just so bad at it.

> *Beat.*

WENDELL: You know…maybe it would be good for us to form a sort of book club.

SAMANTHA: *(Suspicious.)* What would I have to do?

WENDELL: Oh, I'd send you books and you'd read them if you felt like it and then we could talk about them. I think it could be a lot of fun…in fact, I'd enjoy it too.

SAMANTHA: You would?

WENDELL: I'm very interested in what you think about things.

SAMANTHA: What *do* I think about things?

WENDELL: You'll find out! That's what reading is for.

SAMANTHA: …So…you'll just mail me books? For free?

WENDELL: For free. What do you say?

SAMANTHA: I say…yes.

> *The lights shift.*
>
> *A Projection: 1989.*
>
> *A knock on her door. From inside her apartment, JENNY calls out "One minute, Laura!" Then she runs to opens the door.*

JENNY: Oh. You're not–

ADAM: I'm sorry to just come by, I just, I remembered that you lived next-door to Cindy but I'm not here to bother you; I know you don't want anything.

JENNY: No, it's–

ADAM: If you're busy I can come back another time.

JENNY: Sometimes my downstairs neighbor comes over around now to watch TV.

ADAM: …Well if you have one second I could drop off…I mean, I just wanted to bring you some stuff. Well, Brian. I wanted to bring him some books.

JENNY: You brought Brian books?

> *He presents a shopping bag full of books.*

ADAM: You don't have to keep them if you don't want to, but the library is always discarding old books and so I went through them this week and just grabbed a few. I hope that's okay.

JENNY: You didn't have to do this.

ADAM: I know. But…I wanted to.
So—here.

> *He hands her a shopping bag; it's incredibly heavy.*

JENNY: God, how much is in here?

ADAM: I couldn't decide. I didn't know what he'd like.

> *JENNY looks through the bag.*

He'll love *Where the Wild Things Are.*

JENNY: I remember that one. Sorta scary pictures, right? Monsters?

ADAM: *…but Max stepped into his private boat and waved goodbye*
and sailed back over a year
and in and out of weeks
and through a day
and into the night of his very own room

JENNY: You know the whole thing?

ADAM: No. No. Just the relevant passages.

JENNY: Relevant to what?

ADAM: *(Not a joke, deadly serious.)* I don't know. As a kid, I couldn't figure out why, after defeating the Wild Things and becoming their king, Max decides to go back home.

JENNY: You wouldn't have gone back home?

ADAM: Absolutely not.

> *(A breath.)*

JENNY: No. Me neither.

> *(A moment of real connection. A long beat.)*

ADAM: I should really let you watch TV with your friend.

JENNY: Or maybe *you'd* like to watch TV?

> *(Breath. He stares at her.)*

Or do you only read?

ADAM: No…
No, I'm good with TV.

The lights shift.

A Projection: 1975. SAMANTHA is 8.

TRUDY and DOUG sit in WENDELL's office, waiting for him. He enters in a flurry.

WENDELL: I'm so sorry to keep you waiting—Samantha and I were just having such a nice conversation. She was telling me about the birthday party she went to.

TRUDY: Oh yeah, she had a good time. She even wore a dress.

WENDELL: Yes, she told me!

TRUDY: We went shopping for it together. It was fun. We got chocolate ice cream. And tried on all these adorable dresses. She was all "mommy, can I get two?" But I thought one was enough. I mean, it was, right?

WENDELL: Absolutely.

TRUDY: It was a really nice day. I felt really...happy. We both did.

WENDELL: Good.
    Good!

TRUDY: ...but do you think it's a problem that she hasn't been invited to any of the other kids' parties?

WENDELL: Does she seem upset not to be invited?

TRUDY: No. Not really. No. I only learn about it from Stephen. And he says she's just really quiet at school. Like she's not trying very hard to make friends, which I suppose isn't the end of the world? I mean, lord knows I didn't have a lot of friends growing up. My parents moved all over; at a certain point I think I pretty much gave up.

WENDELL: And you still turned out beautifully, didn't you.

TRUDY: *(Blushing.)* Oh, I don't know about that.

WENDELL: To me, in her quiet way, Samantha gets better and better. She's coming into her own. Doug, what have you observed?

DOUG: Me?

WENDELL: Yes. When you two talk, what do you talk about?

> *DOUG and TRUDY look at each other. DOUG doesn't really talk to SAMANTHA.*

DOUG: This and that, I guess.

WENDELL: *(Really putting DOUG on the spot.)* Uh huh.

DOUG: I mean, it's not like we have our own club or anything.

WENDELL: I must admit: I so enjoy my book discussions with Samantha.

DOUG: "The book club."

> *Laughing nervously.*

Me, I've never heard of a two-person club before.

TRUDY: Doug.

WENDELL: Well, I have a lot of favorites. And it brings me so much joy when she reads them.

TRUDY: *I* love it. I have so much on my plate just going down the list of things to do every day–you know, cook with her, play with dolls, watch gymnastics or figure-skating, talk openly and honestly about our bodies–that I wouldn't know how to fit reading in. Plus I'm sure you have smarter things to say about books than we ever would.

> *DOUG doesn't really appreciate that.*

WENDELL: How's that going? The talking about your bodies.

TRUDY: *(It's not going all that well but she covers.)* Oh. Fine!

DOUG: You know, Samantha did this sorta weird thing a couple weeks ago.

WENDELL: And what was that?

TRUDY: I honestly didn't think it was such a big deal.

DOUG: She shaved her face. You know, no shaving cream or anything. Just a razor down her cheek.

TRUDY: *(Jumping in.)* She saw Doug doing it with Stephen. And she felt left out. So when she was on her own she tried it. That's all.

DOUG: There was a lot of blood.

TRUDY: *(Sharp, a little out of nowhere.)* And who cleaned it up?

DOUG: What?

TRUDY: Who drove off with Stephen at nine o'clock at night? Just a little joyride while I'm left with the mess.

WENDELL: I'm sorry—did you say she shaved her face til it bled?

TRUDY: I mean, the other day my cousin Marcy's daughter and one of her little friends were having a tea party where they mixed all these medicines from under the sink. Of course Marcy freaked out, called poison control and they had to take ipecac until they threw up everywhere…I mean, kids will be kids. Right? It's not like this happens with Samantha every day or anything.

WENDELL: And did she seem at all distressed earlier that day?

TRUDY: No. No. From what I saw, she was fine.

WENDELL: You know in future, just drop me a line if something like that happens. I'm sure you're right that it's nothing to worry about but I'd like to be kept up to date on these sorts of things.

TRUDY: All right. But really I don't want to bother you with the small things. You're writing your new book, and talking on the TV. I mean, I was flipping the channels the other day and there you were! I feel like I know a celebrity.

WENDELL: Don't ever worry that you're bothering me. Call anytime. And in the meantime I think the most important thing is to spend time with her. As much as you can.

TRUDY: We do. It's just…you know how life goes. Doug's job is so up and down—

DOUG: My job is fine, thank you very much.

TRUDY: Well, it's not, really. And Stephen's started acting out a bit too.

DOUG: She's just so jealous of him. You can feel it. And so he lords it over her.

WENDELL: She's a classic tomboy.

TRUDY: *(Cutting him off.)* Do you think maybe we should be a little less rigid sometimes? Let her do some of the things that Stephen does? Like Doug is always showing Stephen how the car works, looking under the hood, you know, explaining everything, and Samantha's always dying to be out there too.

WENDELL: Well, you certainly *could* let her join in…but since, on the *whole*, Samantha is doing so well, I wouldn't want to stray too much from the current approach.

TRUDY: Right. Of course.
    So really just stay the course.

WENDELL: I think so. Don't you?

TRUDY: Yes.
    Absolutely.

WENDELL: Doug?

DOUG: *(Not as convinced.)* Oh yeah, absolutely.

> *The lights shift.*
>
> *A Projection: 1989.*
>
> *ADAM and JENNY are in his car. We hear the Back to the Future theme music.*

JENNY: *(Not convincing.)* No, it was good.

ADAM: You liked it?

JENNY: I don't know. Maybe I couldn't remember enough of the first movie? Like, why did Biff hate Marty McFly so much? And: come on. Are there really gonna be such big TVs in the future? I don't think so.

ADAM: Sequels are never as good as the original. But…I still kinda liked it…

JENNY: It was SO nice to have a night out. I hate to say it, but I'm getting tired of Brian and all that growling.

ADAM: Well, a lion has to growl.

JENNY: Oh my god, it's been months. "I'm gonna be a lion when I grow up." Now before bed, I sing him this song about different things you can grow up to be–

ADAM: What song?

JENNY: Oh, um…it's from *Free to be You and Me*, d'you know it?–

ADAM: Sing it.

JENNY: You know…
(She sings quickly, embarrassed.)
Some daddies are writers, or grocery sellers
Or painters or welders, or funny-joke tellers
Some daddies play cello, or sail on the sea
Yeah, daddies can be almost anything they want to be

And at the end he always just goes "I'm gonna be a lion."

ADAM: I can't actually imagine a sweeter thing in the world than you singing to Brian before bed.

An awkward beat.

JENNY: Adam.

ADAM: Should we go? Why don't we go.

JENNY: No, just…

He goes to start the car, but JENNY stops him. She kisses him.

JENNY: Is this okay?

He nods. They keep kissing. She slides her hand up his leg, and as it approaches his groin, he flinches. She moves away from him.

ADAM: I'm sorry–

JENNY: No. I'm sorry.

ADAM: Jenny…

JENNY: *(A guess.)* Is it that you've never kissed anyone before?

ADAM: No…

JENNY: Oh.
Well, are you gay then?

ADAM: What?

JENNY: Last week you came over four nights in a row, played with Brian, read to him for god's sake. And then when he was finally asleep you left. Like you didn't want to be alone with me. And...you sit with your legs crossed in this way that reminds me of this woman who came to teach manners one year at church. You talk a little gay, no offense; you walk a little gay. You read so much.

ADAM: I'm not gay.

JENNY: I mean, if you're not into me, just say it. Lord knows I didn't want to start anything anyway.

ADAM: *(Quietly.)* Okay. If that's what you want.

> *She doesn't say anything.*

But I think about you constantly.

JENNY: Uh-huh.

ADAM: Look, I've had the weirdest week. I read this enormous book. I stayed up all these nights til dawn.

JENNY: You're gonna talk to me about a book now? / Adam?

ADAM: It's not just any book. It's about everything–the beginning of the world–everything. It's actually a poem, the best one ever written, and when I first read it it changed my life, but I hadn't looked at it in so long and all of a sudden I needed to again. Because of you. It's about the fall of man, but now I see that it's also really hopeful. I mean, Adam is nothing for so long; he just listens to everyone, and then when he finally *does* something it triggers the hugest loss mankind has ever known but in the end he and Eve still walk off hand in hand.

JENNY: Okay.

ADAM: So then I was kind of hyper, like high almost–

JENNY: What kind of high?

ADAM: No, not, like...I mean, from not sleeping. But because of the book, too, and somehow I ended up at O'Neill's at three in the morning and I got into a fight with this guy

who was picking on this woman and I told him to stop and
then he took a swing at me and I took a swing back.

JENNY: You got into a fight?

ADAM: And I won. I punched him square in the face.

JENNY: No.

ADAM: And it felt strangely…amazing. I couldn't believe I'd
done it.

JENNY: Oh my God.

ADAM: What?

JENNY: I can't fucking believe myself.

ADAM: What are you talking about?

JENNY: You're just like all the rest of them!

ADAM: The rest of who?

JENNY: Men. The rest of all the men I've ever known.

ADAM: I'm not like them.

JENNY: No?

ADAM: *(Laughing a little.)* No.

JENNY: What's so funny?

ADAM: *(Grounded.)* I just…I love Brian and that Superman
cape he won't take off. I loved when he had chocolate all
over his face and on his arms and he was just licking it off
like a wild animal. I could just watch him do that forever.
I loved chocolate too, as a kid. I would sneak it into my
room and eat Hershey bars in bed, under the covers. I still
crave it sometimes. Don't you?

JENNY: What?

ADAM: Chocolate cake. Chocolate ice cream.
You.

JENNY: I don't know what you want from me. Honestly.

> *Beat.*

ADAM: *(Quietly.)* Will you let me touch you?

I'm touching you right now.
Can you feel it?

JENNY: No.

ADAM: My hand's on your neck, gently, really gently. Just caressing it, really soft and tender. You sure you can't feel it?

> *She shakes her head no. He moves closer to her but isn't touching her.*

ADAM: Now it's on your breast, and I can feel you breathing beneath my hand, and I want to cry, Jenny.

JENNY: *(Quietly, giving in a little.)* Why do you want to cry?

ADAM: I put your breast in my mouth and your heart is in my eyes, beating in me, and you moan a little and I'm like a baby and a man at the same time; I can't get enough, and my other hand is on your stomach and then tangled in your hair and then free as a bird and inside you, and I'm never gonna leave. I'm gonna live there, with your body tucked into mine and mine into yours until I forget I have a body at all, until everything's gone.

JENNY: *(Quietly.)* Adam…

ADAM: Can you feel it?

JENNY: *(Maybe she can, but still–this is so sad.)* I don't know.

> *A Projection: 1978. SAMANTHA is 11.*

> *WENDELL's line summons SAMANTHA into the scene in his office.*

WENDELL: *(Impressed.)* You mean to tell me you read all of *Jane Eyre*? Cover to cover?

SAMANTHA: It only took me two weeks!

WENDELL: Well, that's just amazing. What did you like about it?

SAMANTHA: Oh, um…Jane, I guess?

WENDELL: Yes. She is such a wonderful symbol, isn't she, of independence and freethinking…

SAMANTHA: I didn't think she was a symbol. I thought she was a person.

WENDELL: Of course she is. Of course she is. But she also represents such a refreshing attitude. She feels herself equal to everyone she encounters; in that way, she's a very modern woman, don't you think? "I am no bird; and no net ensnares me: I am a free human being with an independent will."

SAMANTHA: You know the whole book by heart?

WENDELL: No no, only the relevant passages.

SAMANTHA: Wow.

WENDELL: I'm so pleased you read it.

SAMANTHA: Yeah.

I liked it.

WENDELL: By the way, when you were last here, you had a toothache. Has that cleared up?

SAMANTHA: Turned out I had cavities.

WENDELL: How many cavities?

SAMANTHA: Nine.

WENDELL: Nine??

SAMANTHA: So now I have to brush my teeth. They said I have to do it *every day*.

WENDELL: *(Chuckling.)* Yes, I think that would be wise. Maybe your mother could remind you?

SAMANTHA: No, she hates me.

WENDELL: I know for a fact that isn't true.

SAMANTHA: She's always crying because I'm so bad in school.

WENDELL: Well, why do *you* think you're struggling in school?

SAMANTHA: I don't know…I just don't like it.

WENDELL: Does it have to do with the other kids?

      Beat.

Are the other kids not nice to you?

Silence.

Samantha?

SAMANTHA: *(Her voice breaking a bit.)* The books aren't any good, for one thing.

WENDELL: Do you read the books you're assigned in school?

SAMANTHA: No.

WENDELL: Then how do you know they're not good?

SAMANTHA: *(Getting more upset.)*

I just do.

I just do.

WENDELL: *(Going to her and holding her, which leads her to break down.)* Now now. It's really not all that bad, is it?
Is it?

SAMANTHA clings to him.

I know, I know.

It is difficult to be a child. It's so difficult to fit in…I never felt I fit in either. It can be so difficult to be a child.
But you must know it will not always be this way. The lovely thing about life is that we grow up. We do.
And in the meantime, you endure.

SAMANTHA: What does that mean?

WENDELL: It means you carry on.

SAMANTHA: Can I just come live with you?

WENDELL: Live with me?

SAMANTHA: Yeah. Here. In Boston.

Beat.

WENDELL: Well, I don't think your parents would like that very much, do you?

SAMANTHA: They wouldn't care. I talk to you more than I talk to them. More than I talk to anyone. Plus you don't have any children so…

I mean, aren't you lonely?

WENDELL: *(Genuine, bare.)* …Yes. Sometimes.

SAMANTHA: I am too.

And we could read so many books.

> *WENDELL is stricken.*

WENDELL: I wish you could come live with me; I truly do…
But you also have a mom and a dad and they need you as
much as you need them, even if it doesn't always feel that
way.

SAMANTHA: It doesn't.

WENDELL: And anyway, you'd get bored living with me. I
work very long hours; I'm barely ever home.

SAMANTHA: Wouldn't you come home earlier if I was there?

WENDELL: Oh god, how I wish I could wave a magic wand
and erase your unhappiness — but I fear we are up against
greater forces…Which is why I need to bring up the
operation we discussed last year even though I know you
don't want to hear about it.

SAMANTHA: I don't.

WENDELL: We should really do it within the next six or nine
months. I know you don't believe me but it's not fair to *you*
to put it off any longer. I agree: your life is harder than it
needs to be. You need to be made whole. You were born
with a vagina that wasn't quite finished, and you have to
have one that's fully functioning. And you have to trust me
that *this* will make all the difference.

> *SAMANTHA doesn't say anything.*

WENDELL: *(So gently.)* Will you say something, Samantha?
Will you let me know you've heard me?

SAMANTHA: *(Quietly.)* I've heard you.

> *A Projection: 1990.*

> *ADAM and JENNY and TRUDY sit in the Turner living-room.*

TRUDY: Well isn't this nice.

Just the three of us. Two gals and a guy, sitting around.

Hey, would you two like another beer? There's lots more.

JENNY: I'm okay, thanks.

ADAM: Sure, I'll have another beer. Why not.

TRUDY: Great! Maybe I'll get myself one too. Don't mind if I do, you know. This is such a nice occasion.

> *TRUDY goes.*

JENNY: This is weird.

ADAM: She loves you.

JENNY: You think?

ADAM: You're doing great.

JENNY: I don't know.

ADAM: I do.

> *He puts his hand on JENNY's leg and leaves it there, conspicuously, possessively. TRUDY returns, gives ADAM his beer.*

TRUDY: There you go.

> *Beat.*

Like I was saying, this is so nice. A little strange, but so, so nice.

JENNY: Why is it strange?

TRUDY: No—I just mean, seeing Adam with…someone. Don't get me wrong—it's really so nice. I mean, I don't even mind that we never see him anymore. He was usually only coming over to do his laundry anyway.

JENNY: That's what my mom was always saying about me.

TRUDY: Gosh, it's so hard to live without a washer-dryer, isn't it? We had an apartment right when Stephen and…right when my babies were born and we had to drag these huge bags all the way to the Laundromat every other day. It felt like I lived there.

JENNY: Adam doesn't like to stay and wait while the clothes are in the machine. He thinks men don't do that.

TRUDY: Is that right?

ADAM: I never said that.

JENNY: You've said that so many times.

ADAM: *(Annoyed.)* Where's dad?

TRUDY: Working late, I imagine.

ADAM: Least he could have done would have been to come home. To meet Jenny.

TRUDY: Well, to be fair you didn't give us too much advance notice.

ADAM: *(Frustrated.)* How much advance notice do you need that I'm in love?

TRUDY: That's such a sweet thing to hear you say.

ADAM: *(Sharply.)* Well, it's true.

JENNY: You don't sound too happy about it.

ADAM: You know I'm happy.

TRUDY: This is just how he gets.

ADAM: Don't tell her how I get.

TRUDY: *(Trying to be measured.)* I'm sorry, I didn't mean to–

JENNY: *(Trying to bring thing back on track.)* Hey–tell me what Adam was like as a kid. Like, tell me a story about him.

TRUDY: What kind of story?

JENNY: I don't know. My mom was always saying my sister and me were as bad as twins so I bet actual twins got up to some mischief.

> *Turning, subtly, to ADAM.*

TRUDY: She doesn't know?

JENNY: What don't I know?

> *ADAM doesn't say anything for a beat.*

ADAM: *(Quietly.)* Let's just move on.

TRUDY: Okay. Yes! I'm all for moving on. I think the past is the past and doesn't need to be dredged up all the time.

ADAM: *(Sullenly.)* Right.

TRUDY: Because you can't undo it, can you. As much as you might want to. And lord knows I want to, but there it is. So you either spend your life sitting on top of that huge, growing mountain or you move on from it and then, eventually, you see that peak getting smaller behind you.

ADAM: It's easy for you to say if your mountain isn't made of shit.

TRUDY: Adam…

JENNY: Maybe I should go.

ADAM: No. We have to stay. We have to stay and you have to meet my dad. And we all have to have a beer together. That was the whole point. For us to sit together and just… For you and dad to see me with Jenny, for you to see how much I love her and how much she loves me, but now it's all fucked up. It's just gotten all fucked up.

JENNY: *(Standing.)* It was nice to meet you.

TRUDY: You too. You really are a nice girl. I can tell.

ADAM: She's a woman for god's sakes. She has a child. Jesus Christ.

TRUDY: Oh, you have a child?

JENNY: I wasn't, um. I wasn't going to…

ADAM: And he's adorable. Just adorable.

TRUDY: Where's his dad?

ADAM: The dad's a deadbeat–

JENNY: Adam–

ADAM: He is. He's an asshole. I'll be Brian's dad.

JENNY: What?

ADAM: No…I mean…I just mean maybe I'd do a better job. If it came to that.

TRUDY: Gosh, sweetheart, you can't just offer to be someone's dad. A lot of stuff has to happen before you do that.

ADAM: Don't you think I know that! I know that.

TRUDY: Being a dad isn't just about playing little games, and—

ADAM: You think I'm five, don't you.

But I'm twenty-three years old!

TRUDY: I know that.

ADAM: And playing games with little kids is a heck of a lot better than some other things you could do to them.

> *He starts to leave; he doesn't want JENNY to see him cry.*

JENNY: Adam—

> *JENNY makes to follow him.*

ADAM: Stay away from me!

> *He exits into the scene with WENDELL.*

TRUDY: No…Let him go.

WENDELL: Oh, that is an excellent move…Gosh, I think you've nearly got me cornered.

TRUDY: *(Quietly, almost to herself.)* You know the crazy thing is…I actually miss her sometimes.

JENNY: Miss who?

TRUDY: *(Sadly, quietly.)* No one.

> *TRUDY shakes her head, sadly. The lights shift.*
>
> *A Projection: 1979. SAMANTHA is 12.*
>
> *WENDELL and SAMANTHA play chess, seated across a table from one another. SAMANTHA moves a piece. She is very combative in this scene, sullen. Not trying to please him.*

WENDELL: Let me see if there's any way out of this for me… Do you see a way out?

SAMANTHA: You're letting me win.

WENDELL: No I'm not.

SAMANTHA nods.

That was an excellent move.

WENDELL moves.

Ah. But I did find a way to stay alive a little longer.

SAMANTHA moves.

You sure you want to do that?

SAMANTHA shrugs.

Okay. Well…then I'm going to get your queen.

He does.

Did you do that on purpose—expose your queen?

SAMANTHA: I don't want to play anymore.

WENDELL: Why not?

SAMANTHA: You win. I lose. Game over.

SAMANTHA stands.

WENDELL: What's wrong?

SAMANTHA: Why do you let me beat you at chess?

WENDELL: I told you—I'm not letting you beat me.

SAMANTHA: And why'd you send me that book? I hated it. It was so boring. And it's for little kids. I wanna read more Narnia.

WENDELL: You might've hated it but it's not a book for little children. *Are You There God, It's Me Margaret* is absolutely age-appropriate. Also you've read all the Narnia books. There are no more.

SAMANTHA: I saw *Star Wars* two times on Saturday. My mom said she would kill me if I stayed and watched it again. And so I watched it again.

WENDELL: Did you. And were you there with a friend?

SAMANTHA: No.

WENDELL: Stephen then?

SAMANTHA: No.

WENDELL: You were at the movies by yourself?

SAMANTHA: I wish I was Luke Skywalker.

WENDELL: *(Hopeful.)* You mean you find him attractive? You have a little crush on him?

SAMANTHA: I don't have a crush on him.

WENDELL: He is quite dashing, I suppose.

SAMANTHA: No! I want to be Luke Skywalker. *Be* him.

WENDELL: Are you all right, Samantha? You seem…You don't really seem yourself.

SAMANTHA: I don't know what that means. I am always myself.

WENDELL: All right, yes. But a rather obstinate version today, perhaps. "Obstinate" means stubborn.

SAMANTHA: I don't care.

WENDELL: I don't think you really wish to *be* this character.

> *Then a genuine question.*

Do you?

SAMANTHA: I do.

WENDELL: *(Slowly, treading carefully.)* And…what is it about this character that makes you want to be…him?

SAMANTHA: Just everything about him.

WENDELL: Everything about him.

SAMANTHA: Yeah.

WENDELL: *(At a loss.)* Okay, so…

SAMANTHA: Okay?

> *WENDELL's face betrays some uncertainty.*

WENDELL: And did you…have you, um…felt this way about other characters?

> *Beat.*

Did you feel that way about Jane Eyre maybe?

SAMANTHA: No. I mean, I liked Jane.

WENDELL: Right.

SAMANTHA: We had stuff in common.

WENDELL: *(Grabbing onto this.)* Ah. Yes. You related to her!

SAMANTHA: Yeah, maybe.

WENDELL: She's so headstrong and free.

SAMANTHA: No, just that her life is so sad.

> *Beat.*

WENDELL: *(Carefully, gently.)* Samantha…is your life really so sad?

> *SAMANTHA doesn't say anything.*

I just…I don't want you to…how should I put this…I don't want you to want things you can't have, or which would be very difficult to achieve. And so I want to make sure I am really hearing you.

SAMANTHA: Are you going deaf or something?

WENDELL: No. No I'm not going deaf.

I am, in fact, listening really hard. And also observing really hard.

SAMANTHA: Observing me.

WENDELL: Right. And sometimes what I hear doesn't always square with what I see. And I have to get to the bottom of that.

SAMANTHA: What do you see?

WENDELL: I see…this lovely girl.

A lovely girl who doesn't believe she has the power to shape her own reality. A girl who sometimes chafes against things because they seem difficult when in fact difficult things can be good for us, in the end.

SAMANTHA: I don't want to talk about the operation if that's what you're talking about.

WENDELL: Well…I'm sure it's uncomfortable to know that we remain in disagreement. But please understand that it doesn't mean I think any less of you. I am still your friend.

SAMANTHA: Just let it go. I'm not gonna do it.

WENDELL: So you've said. And *I* will continue to argue that it's very important.

SAMANTHA: How do you know?

WENDELL: What?

SAMANTHA: How do you know that it's important. That it would be so good for me.

WENDELL: I know it's important in the same way I know that it's important that you take your medicine so that your breasts develop.

SAMANTHA: *(Abrupt, violent, despairing.)* Don't talk about those! I don't have them. What you said. I don't have them.

WENDELL: Well, you do, a little. Just the beginnings of—

SAMANTHA: Stop it!! Just stop talking.

WENDELL: Samantha!

SAMANTHA: I'm sorry.

I'm sorry.

WENDELL: What's come over you?

SAMANTHA: I don't know!

> *She cries.*

I don't know…

WENDELL: *(Quietly.)* Samantha. My dear.

SAMANTHA: I just…I hate you.

> *Beat.*

WENDELL: *(Quietly, gently, hurt.)* You don't mean that. Do you?

SAMANTHA: *(In despair.)* No.

WENDELL: I promise I wasn't letting you win. Come on, let's see if you can beat me. Fair and square.

SAMANTHA: *(Quietly.)* I can't beat you.

WENDELL: Of course you can.

> *The lights shift.*
>
> *A Projection: 1980. SAMANTHA is 13.*
>
> *WENDELL knocks on the Turners' front door. TRUDY opens it.*

TRUDY: Oh. Dr. –   WENDELL: Trudy, hello! It's so
                                       lovely to see you.

TRUDY: Did I know you were in town?

WENDELL: I was at a conference not too far away, so I figured I'd drop in and say hello.

TRUDY: Oh.

> *Beat. She stands there, frozen.*

WENDELL: Can I come in?

TRUDY: Oh. Um–yes. Come in, of course come in.

> *TRUDY makes way for WENDELL to enter and he does.*

Gosh, I'm sorry it's such a mess. I wasn't expecting anyone.

WENDELL: It's perfect.

TRUDY: Can I get you something? A beer? Or Coffee?

WENDELL: Sure, coffee would be welcome.

TRUDY: Just gimme a sec.

> *She exits. WENDELL stands, not sure what to do with his hands. He rearranges some magazines on the table. He's nervous. TRUDY returns, holding a beer.*

I'm so sorry–we're out of coffee. I hoped, that is I thought we–

WENDELL: A beer would be fine.

TRUDY: Oh good.

> *She hands it to WENDELL. It's a can. His distaste is evident but he goes ahead and opens it and takes a reluctant sip.*

Do you want to sit?

> *She clears a place on the couch, moving newspapers and magazines and coupons to make room. He sits. TRUDY sits. An awkward beat.*

TRUDY: Well, this is such a nice surprise.

WENDELL: I couldn't come so close and not check in on my favorite family, could I. They are home, aren't they—the twins?

TRUDY: The twins? Um, yes.

WENDELL: Especially after you missed your appointment a couple weeks ago. And I've been calling.

TRUDY: I'm sorry—we just couldn't…we couldn't get there. I'm so sorry I didn't call.

WENDELL: I've been worried.

TRUDY: Dr. Barnes. Wendell…Can I talk with you, just frankly?…Just…frankly?

WENDELL: About what?

TRUDY: Well…we've been…we've been having trouble… lately. You see, Samantha doesn't seem to be taking to… And I wondered if there was anything else we could…

WENDELL: What part of things is she not taking to?

TRUDY: The whole being a girl part?

WENDELL: It's a long process, Trudy. Full of ups and downs.

TRUDY: No, I know, I just want to be sure you still feel…sure.

WENDELL: Do I feel sure?

TRUDY: Right.

WENDELL: I feel…that teenagers act out. That's what teenagers do.

TRUDY: Well, yes.

WENDELL: Can I see her? I'd really like to see her now.

TRUDY: I don't know.

WENDELL: Please.

TRUDY: Okay, let me…I'll just go tell them you're here.

WENDELL: I'll come with you.

TRUDY: *(A bit too abruptly.)* No–

> *She catches herself.*

I mean, that's all right. I'll go.

> *She leaves; he waits. He waits a long time and gets impatient. He takes another sip of beer and is repulsed by it. She finally returns. He looks at her, searchingly.*

I'm so sorry…You came all the way here, and…

WENDELL: And what?

TRUDY: Well I'm afraid the twins aren't available right now.

WENDELL: What could thirteen year olds conceivably be doing that would make them unavailable?

TRUDY: Like I said–I'm sorry.

WENDELL: *(Slowly, piecing it together.)* You don't want her to see me. You've given up.

TRUDY: That's not it. I tried. I really did. I want her to see you.

WENDELL: Then let me go down there.

> *He starts towards the stairs and TRUDY physically blocks him.*

TRUDY: I can't let you do that. She's too upset.

WENDELL: All the more reason I should see her. Please.

> *DOUG arrives home.*

DOUG: What's going on here??

TRUDY: *(Containing herself again.)* Dr. Barnes is here.

DOUG: I see that. Why?

WENDELL: I was in town, and so I stopped by. I hope that's all right.

DOUG: Well, actually. Well, actually, no. It's not all right.

WENDELL: And why's that? We've never had a problem before.

DOUG: Oh no? We've never had any problems?

WENDELL: Are you ok, Doug?

DOUG: Don't call me Doug.

WENDELL: I'm sorry—

DOUG: I don't like walking in here and seeing you.

WENDELL: Where is this coming from? Trudy?

TRUDY: I...um.

WENDELL: I saw Samantha just a few months ago. Maybe she was a little blue, but nothing out of bounds for a girl her age.

DOUG: Did you know whenever she visits you she spends that night bawling her eyes out? Did you know that?

WENDELL: I know she's sad when we have to say goodbye. But I don't think it's an unhealthy attachment. I've known her all her life.

DOUG: Right, she worships you. And it tortures her.

WENDELL: Will you tell me what's happened to Samantha since I saw her?

TRUDY: She hasn't left her room. She won't go to school.

WENDELL: What? Why didn't you tell me?

TRUDY: She didn't want me to.

WENDELL: I don't understand.

DOUG: She doesn't want an operation, okay?

WENDELL: Well, I know that. But who *wants* an operation?

DOUG: *(Under his breath.)* Jesus.

TRUDY: *(Quietly.)* I think Doug's trying to say that over the years, we put on sort of a brave face.

WENDELL: I appreciate your candor, but I am, also, you must remember, a doctor. I've observed Samantha all these years.

TRUDY: *(Quietly.)* Samantha in particular. I think Samantha in particular put on a brave face.

WENDELL: Why would she do that?

DOUG: Why would she do that? You're really asking?

WENDELL: *(Not as firm as he'd like.)* I am.

DOUG: Because she wants to please you! She's desperate to be your good little girl. But she's not, really. Is she. She doesn't fit in with anyone. Hates wearing girl's clothes. Stands up to pee. Did you know that? She stands. What girl does that? Trudy says she won't wear her little bra; no, she claws at herself to try to make her you-know-whats go away. She won't do her schoolwork. Too depressed. Too lonely. She's thirteen years old and no one talks to her. Not even her brother, and they used to be friends.

> *TRUDY puts her head in her hands in shame and misery.*

WENDELL: It's upsetting for all of us that she's been going through such a rough patch.

DOUG: *(Exploding now.)* All these years, it's "a rough patch"; it's "kids being kids"; it's "she's a tomboy"–

TRUDY: Doug, why don't you settle down a bit…

DOUG: Why don't you shut up, Trudy!

WENDELL: If you want to take my words entirely out of context–

DOUG: Oh, come on, we both know you never really cared about Sam. All you wanted was a doll to play dress-up with. To prove your theories with.

WENDELL: No. I care about Samantha. Deeply. Terribly.

DOUG: Well, I'm her father!

WENDELL: *(He can't help himself.)* Then act like it!…Pay her some attention…To be honest, I'm not sure either of you pays her the kind of attention she needs.

DOUG: *(To TRUDY.)* This is hilarious. Isn't this hilarious?

WENDELL: I really think we ought to focus on Samantha and what we can do to help her feel she can go to school again. Can we do that? Can we focus?

DOUG: Oh no, *we* aren't gonna do anything.

WENDELL: What does that mean?

DOUG: It means you aren't gonna have anything to do with Samantha anymore. It means I'd like you to get out of my house.

WENDELL: Please don't do this. Please. Consider Samantha. What would she think if I just…disappeared? It would be a devastating blow. It would shape her. She needs me.

TRUDY: *(Cutting him off.)* Samantha said she won't see you! And I'm at my wit's end…I just can't force her to do things anymore…I can't do it.

WENDELL: *(In shock.)* Samantha said that? That she didn't want to see me?
I don't believe it.
I don't believe you.

TRUDY: *(In a sudden burst.)* Maybe it didn't work! Did you ever consider that? That maybe it didn't work??

> *Then she realizes what she's articulated aloud.*

Oh god, maybe it didn't work.

> *Even quieter.*

Oh my god.

> *Quieter still.*

Oh my god.

WENDELL: No, she's going through a rough patch.
A rough patch. You'll see. She's gonna be fine. She's gonna be just fine.

TRUDY: *(Quietly.)* You need to go Dr. Barnes.

WENDELL: Trudy?

DOUG: Go.

The lights shift.

A Projection: 1990.

It's a few hours after the date-gone-wrong at ADAM's parents' house. We are in ADAM's home. ADAM sits, drinking. He's had a few already. He's being very cold to JENNY, detached.

JENNY: *(Indicating the drinking.)* You wanna stop now.

ADAM: Nope.

JENNY: Okay, well then I think I'm gonna go.

ADAM: Fine.

JENNY: Fine.

She stands to go.

You're really gonna take this out on me?

ADAM: Take what out on you?

JENNY: I *liked* what you said about being Brian's dad. That made me happy.

ADAM: *(Skeptically.)* Uh-huh.

JENNY: But your mom might be right that…well, just that we should give it a lot of thought. Not rush into anything.

ADAM: No, wouldn't want to rush into anything.

JENNY: I hate this.

ADAM: You didn't take time to think with the others, did you.

JENNY: What?

ADAM: "Does he have two legs? Check. And a heartbeat? Check…Well! I guess that's good enough for me."

JENNY: That's enough.

ADAM: Well, how is it supposed to make me feel? You tell me and I'll feel that way.

JENNY: So I can't start over? That's not allowed for me?

ADAM: Sure. Start over. But for some reason I still feel shitty about all the men you've fucked.

JENNY: You just expect me to like you no matter what you say to me!

ADAM: I don't expect anything from you.

JENNY: Then, you know what? Go fuck yourself.

ADAM: What?

JENNY: Go fuck yourself and your dome light and your secrets and your weird shit with women.

ADAM: What weird shit with women?

JENNY: *(Like a dam bursting.)* You won't fuck me, Adam!! I mean, that's maybe just a little bit weird, isn't it??

ADAM: That's not fair.

JENNY: No, what's not fair is you saying "guess what. Tomorrow we're having dinner with my parents" and me running out to get a new dress because everything I have is gross and then we're there with your mom and you just take off. So you know what? Fuck all of it.

> *She sits, with her head in her hands; she's nearly crying.*

JENNY: *(Quietly.)* All I've been is nice to you.

ADAM: But I deserve more than that. Don't I?

JENNY: What? What do you deserve?

ADAM: I don't know…

JENNY: Who gets anything they deserve, anyway? Does anyone? I mean, I look at Brian and hope to god he's not looking back at me. Because one day he'll either judge me or follow in my footsteps, and neither one of those is even remotely okay. But what can I do? I don't have the luxury to just be weird and unhappy.

ADAM: I'm not just *unhappy*…

JENNY: Then what are you?

> *Beat, then searchingly.*

I mean…what happened to you??

ADAM: What?

JENNY: What happened to you?

ADAM: Don't badger me, okay?

JENNY: Who does your mom miss?? Some ex-girlfriend? Maybe a wife? No don't give me that look—I've been there. I've been there.

ADAM: You think *your* life's been hard?

JENNY: What's been so hard about your life, Adam? Jesus God. Just tell me already.

ADAM: I honestly don't know what you're...

JENNY: Yes you do.

> *Beat.*

You do.

ADAM: *(Desperate.)* I love you so much. I love you more than I've loved anybody in my entire life.

JENNY: I don't believe you anymore.

ADAM: I don't know. It's like a war, maybe...

JENNY: What war. What are you talking about?

ADAM: Like maybe there were soldiers and they were captured and there was a guard who fed them and gave them what they needed but also, everyday, he cut off a piece of them.

JENNY: You're not making any sense.

ADAM: I just...I can't.

JENNY: Don't make me do this.

ADAM: Then don't.

JENNY: Oh god are you an asshole.

ADAM: Please. Jenny.

> *Beat, and then decisively.*

JENNY: No.

I've had enough.

> *She leaves. The lights shift.*

A Projection: One Week Later

ADAM's doorbell rings. ADAM doesn't answer it. It rings again. It keeps ringing. Finally, DOUG opens the unlocked door and enters, standing just inside.

DOUG: Getting hard of hearing in your old age?

ADAM: What're you doing here.

DOUG: You really hafta ask?...Your mom sent me.
    She's been calling you.

ADAM: She has?

DOUG: Oh you know she has. That woman has worried about you every day of your life, kid, and that'll never stop...
    So you gonna invite me in?

ADAM: Do I have a choice?

> *DOUG enters, holding a cooler. He sits, the cooler next to him. He opens it, takes out a beer.*

DOUG: You want one?

> *ADAM shakes his head no.*

No? I'll drink for the both of us then.

> *He opens his beer.*

You know I was just telling Stephen the other day...I said, the funny thing about people, they don't know what they need...or if they do, they don't go out and get it...For me it was only when I hit the big 4-0, when I realized half my life was probably behind me, that I bought this little cooler. That way, I can always have a cold beer on hand, which is a little thing but also it isn't, you know?

> *ADAM doesn't say anything. DOUG drinks, and then laughs quietly to himself.*

See, that's your mom for you. Always sending me to do her dirty work...I shoulda known from the second I met your mother that I'd be doing her bidding the rest of my life...I guess I still woulda signed up for it, though.

ADAM: *(Weirded out.)* Okay.

Beat.

DOUG: I know we don't really talk, and I'm sorry for that. I am. I mean, at least your mother tried, right? You've gotta give her credit. She never gives up, whereas I give up, just like that. Always have. Some would probably say that's why my record of employment isn't exactly "pristine."

ADAM: Dad–

DOUG: You know, I have this memory. You were eight maybe, couldn't have been much more than eight, and your mom is making your lunch and you turn to her and say: "why do you always make me peanut butter and jelly? I don't like peanut butter and I *despise* jelly." You said it that way–*despise*–as though you were the queen of England or something. My kid. I mean, where did you come from? I never said "despise"–not once in my life.

ADAM: I didn't really say that. I'm sure I didn't.

DOUG: Yeah, none of us really knows ourselves all that well, do we…

ADAM: What do you mean?

DOUG: If I could live one day over and over again, I know which one it'd be. Easy.
You and Stephen just babies, six months old. Not sleeping at all. Not a wink. I get home from work six in the AM and your mother's wiped out. Just gray in the face she's so tired. And so I tell her go to bed. Usually I go to sleep when I get home, see, but this time, I saw how gone she was and so I took you and your brother and strapped you in the car and we went for a ride. I went straight to the lakes and we drove around and around until the sun was up. You two fell asleep straightaway. And after a little while I look into the backseat, and I kid you not, your hand was on your brother's head, just resting there, as though you intended to protect him the rest of your life.

ADAM: What're you doing, dad?

DOUG: You know, I think you came out of your mother just who you are. This kind, gentle boy.

Beat.

ADAM: So it's over with Jenny.

Breath.

DOUG: Is that right?

ADAM: Yeah.

DOUG: And why's that?

ADAM shakes his head.

You know…women need you to reveal yourself to them. You gotta pretend you have something only they can know. Come up with a secret and then tell it. That's the way I got your mother, I think. Made her feel she was the only one who could know me. And kept enough of myself to myself to keep her guessing at the same time. Over all these years.

ADAM: Tell her I'm sorry I haven't called, okay?

DOUG: Okay.

ADAM: You know you shouldn't drink so much, dad.

DOUG: I know that.

But sometimes we just can't control what it is we do, can we.

The lights shift. ADAM is arriving home and there's WENDELL, on his doorstep. For a moment, ADAM can't speak; the breath has been knocked out of him.

WENDELL: Oh, I'm sorry, do you live here?

I'm just waiting for someone.

ADAM: *(Surprised.)* You don't recognize me.

WENDELL: What?

He studies him.

No…it can't be. Is it…is it Stephen?

Beat.

ADAM: Yeah, it's me. Stephen.

WENDELL: Do you and Samantha both live here?

A breath.

ADAM: *(Quietly, not sure where this will go.)* Yeah. Me and
   Samantha...

WENDELL: My god, Stephen. I haven't seen you in...

ADAM: Ten years.

WENDELL: You're a grown man now.

ADAM: I am?

WENDELL: Would you mind telling me when Samantha might
   be home?

   A breath.

ADAM: I don't know.

WENDELL: She wrote to me. I came as soon as I could.

   A breath, then quietly.

   I've missed her so.

ADAM: You have?

WENDELL: Terribly.

   Beat. ADAM is moved and confused.

   I didn't think I'd hear from her again. But then there it
   was. A letter containing one sentence. *I need you to see me.*
   This address. And I realized that all along we've been on
   the same page. Needing each other. And I felt very foolish
   for not making contact much sooner.

ADAM: So you've been...

WENDELL: Trying to keep busy. Not teaching quite so much.
   Not publishing quite so much.

ADAM: Why not?

WENDELL: Oh, I don't know. At a certain stage, a kind of
   fatigue sets in maybe. You feel you've made your point;
   you've been heard, and maybe you don't need to keep
   making it.

   Breath.

ADAM: Yeah, you look older…

WENDELL: I'm sorry, but do you expect your sister home anytime soon?

ADAM: My brother you mean.

WENDELL: Well…maybe in a manner of speaking–

ADAM: *(Gently.)* No, not in a manner of speaking. In reality. In the world.

> *A breath.*

WENDELL: Where is she, Stephen? Is she okay?

ADAM: *(Quietly.)* No she's not okay.

WENDELL: She's not.

ADAM: She never felt she fit in with anyone. She's not a girl; she's not a boy; she's not a grown up; she's not a child.

WENDELL: Is she…does she have many friends?…A boyfriend? A job she enjoys?

ADAM: No. None of those things.

WENDELL: I need to see her.
When will your sister be home?

> *ADAM reaches into a pocket and pulls out a wallet. From it he removes a folded piece of paper and shoves it at WENDELL.*

ADAM: Here.

WENDELL: What's this?

ADAM: Read it.

> *WENDELL begins to read to himself.*

ADAM: Out loud.

WENDELL: *(Reading.)* Dear Wendell, here's something I never told you. When we were kids, Stephen and me, we shared a room. You didn't want that, but my parents couldn't afford a bigger house, so that's the way it was.

> *WENDELL looks up but ADAM motions that he continue.*

And I remember all these nights, too many to count, when we were going to sleep and Stephen maybe thought I was asleep already or maybe he didn't give a shit, and he was ten maybe eleven when it started.

ADAM: Keep going.

WENDELL: I watched him; I saw how everything worked. How his dick would get hard in his hand, how he caressed it like it was the softest sweetest thing in the world and then how he fought it, like an animal trying to break free. And when he came, I swear I felt it too…this sensation of almost being somewhere and needing to get there, desperately, but…I'd look down–and there was nothing there.

ADAM: Keep going.

Keep going!

WENDELL: Once you asked me when I grew up whether I wanted to marry a boy or a girl. And I said a boy. But it's not true; it was never true. I wanted girls from the earliest moments I can remember. Even when they wouldn't talk to me. When no one would talk to me. Except you. Even then I wanted girls. But I couldn't find a way to tell you. Plus I think I saw myself through your eyes–after all, only you saw something good in me, all those years. Even though you didn't really see *me*.

ADAM: My name is Adam.

I chose my name. I chose it.

See, I was never Samantha. She never existed. She was just a piece of fiction like all the books you ever sent me.

WENDELL: No she wasn't.

ADAM: Look at me, Wendell.

He doesn't.

I said look at me!

WENDELL: Don't do this.

ADAM: My whole childhood, Wendell. My whole childhood.

WENDELL: So what do you want me to say? That I knew? That I was intentionally hurting you?

ADAM: Say you never cared about me. Say all you wanted was the experiment to be a success. Say it was all about your career. Making a name for yourself.

WENDELL: But you know it's not true.

ADAM: It has to be true.

WENDELL: No, I helped people. I know I did. I helped you. I saw it with my own eyes. And *you* helped people. The success of your case…

ADAM: But I wasn't just a case. An example for *science*!

WENDELL: No, you weren't. I believed in you. I believed in you…And I cared about you as though you were my own child. You know I did. I do.

ADAM: You loved her. Not *me*. And you were everything to me. Do you know what that did to me? What it's still doing to me? I don't know who I am.

WENDELL: *(Impossibly sad, desperate.)* Samantha.

ADAM: That's not my name. Say my name.

WENDELL: Sam. Samantha.

ADAM: No. Say *my* name. Say *my* name.

> *Desperate and sad.*

Say it. Please. *Please* say it, Wendell.

WENDELL: Adam.

ADAM: Say it again.

WENDELL: Adam.

ADAM: Thank you.

> *ADAM goes to WENDELL and takes or touches his hand or arm.*

Now promise you'll never see me again. Ever. And you have to keep your promise.

WENDELL: I can't.

ADAM: *(With real urgency/need.)* You have to.

WENDELL: *(Quietly, his heart breaking.)* Okay. I promise.

> *A Projection: 1990. Halloween.*

> *The doorbell rings. WENDELL exits. ADAM answers the door. It's JENNY, in costume, as Clark Kent. She is wary around ADAM, trying not to get too close, too familiar.*

JENNY: Hey.

ADAM: Hey.

JENNY: *(Coldly.)* So. Why'd you want to see me?

ADAM: *(Laughing.)* Why are you dressed like that?

JENNY: I just came from trick-or-treating with Brian. It's Halloween.

ADAM: It is?

JENNY: He still wouldn't take off that stupid Superman cape, so I decided what the hell I'd be Clark Kent.

ADAM: So you think Clark Kent had a mustache?

> *He removes the stick-on mustache from over her lip.*

JENNY: I don't know. Didn't he?

> *They both hold their breath; it's gotten very intimate very quickly.*

ADAM: Have you ever been with a girl?

JENNY: Excuse me??

ADAM: You asked once if I'd ever kissed anyone before. And I said I had. But the truth is I'd never kissed a girl before.

JENNY: So, what, you kissed a boy?

ADAM: Once I did.

JENNY: What?

ADAM: 8th grade prom. This kid Billy Hoffstedter asked me to go with him. And I didn't want to go but I knew it would make my mom happy if I did. And so I put on my party dress and my party shoes and off we went. And we danced a little. And I was mortified. And then I went to the bathroom, and he followed me. He kind of led me around the corner into this dark hallway. And then he kissed me. He put his hands on my chest—I had a chest then because of the hormones and everything—and it was just awful. Just the worst thing that had ever happened to me in a long line of bad things that happened to me. And I didn't push him off. I just let him do it.

Beat.

JENNY: Billy Hoffstedter went to my school.

ADAM: He went to mine too.

She stares at him; then she realizes.

JENNY: Oh my god.

ADAM just nods. She knows who he is.

Oh my god.

ADAM: I was born a boy, but there was an accident, and then for fifteen years I was a girl, not knowing I'd been anything else, but also knowing, you know? And after that, I was a boy again, and I had three operations, and now I have a dick that doesn't really work. Not really.

Beat.

Yeah for fifteen years I didn't know. Until this one afternoon. I came home from not being at school, which wasn't unusual, and the school had called to see where I was, so my mom was waiting for me in the living-room. "Where were you all day?" she asked, and she was crying. My mom, my poor mom.
And I think that's when she decided it hadn't worked.
So it wasn't a special day or anything. Just a day like all the others that made her finally give in.

And that night she told my dad to take me out for ice cream. But after we got it we sat in the car, in silence, and he didn't start the engine. His hands were shaking and he said, "there's something I need to tell you." And he told me everything. And my father cried. And I had never seen him cry before. And he called me "son." And then we realized the ice cream had melted all over us so we went back into the store to get some more. It's funny, I remember that, that we went back in and got some more.

Beat.

JENNY: What flavor was it?

ADAM: ...Chocolate.

JENNY: Chocolate, huh.

ADAM: Yeah.

JENNY: *(Quietly.)* Sometimes I just crave chocolate, don't you?

ADAM: Yeah.

(They make eye contact.)

ADAM: *(Quietly.)* That was the night I was born.

JENNY: So how old does that make you now?

ADAM: Oh, I guess that'd make me...just about eight.

JENNY: Eight...eight... I don't know eight that well...Does that mean you want to watch cartoons?

ADAM: No.

JENNY: Do you want to pretend I'm a dinosaur and tell me I can't make you take a shower because I'm extinct and extinct things can't talk?

ADAM: No.

JENNY: Do you want me to read to you?

He smiles.

Okay, what should I read?

A breath.

ADAM: I memorized one thing when I was growing up. I didn't even mean to but I saw it a lot and it just stuck. And I realized why when I walked into that party. It was just– BAM. There you were, in second grade again, sitting in the corner by the aquarium, which made your whole face glow.

JENNY: *(Quietly.)* I used to just stare and stare at those fish.

ADAM: I used to stare and stare at you.

JENNY: You didn't.

ADAM: You invited me to your birthday party. You volunteered to be my partner for the research paper, when no one else would.

JENNY: I liked you. There was something about you.

ADAM: That's why I remembered this poem all these years.

JENNY: A poem.

ADAM: It's about you.

JENNY: What do you mean it's about me?

ADAM: *(Reciting it in a whisper.)*
Jenny kissed me when we met,
Jumping from the chair she sat in.
Time, you thief! who love to get
Sweets into your list, put that in.
Say I'm weary, say I'm sad;
Say that health and wealth have missed me;
Say I'm growing old, but add-
Jenny kissed me!

> *ADAM grabs JENNY and kisses her; it's intense.*

See…it's about you. And me.

> *(JENNY kisses ADAM. She puts her hands under his shirt, starts to pull it up. They kiss gently, tenderly as the lights fade.)*

THE LAST MATCH

Characters

TIM

mid-30s, a professional tennis player, all-American; he is even-keeled, slightly arrogant, charming and incredibly likeable; he knows how to get the crowd on his side

SERGEI

mid-20s, a Russian professional tennis player; he wears his heart on his sleeve; he's wild and unruly and funny and untamed

MALLORY

mid-30s, Tim's wife and a former player; she's level-headed, calm, with an easy laugh and sarcastic sense of humor

GALINA

mid/late 20s, Sergei's girlfriend, also Russian; she's fiery and no-nonsense; you wouldn't want to mess with her but not far beneath the surface are the vulnerabilities that make her who she is

Setting

The semifinals of the U.S. Open. Sort of.

Note

The play is made up of scenes inside the tennis match and memories that take place outside of it. As much as possible, transitions from one to the other should seamlessly blur these boundaries, so that, for instance, the line of dialogue that serves as the bridge from one kind of scene to the other feels that it applies to both worlds.

The Last Match was originally produced by The Old Globe Theatre in San Diego, California (Barry Edelstein, Artistic Director) on February 18, 2016. The director was Gaye Taylor Upchurch, the stage manager Diana Moser, the set designer Tim Mackabee, the costume designer Denitsa Bliznakova, the lighting designer Bradley King, and the sound designer Bray Poor. The cast was as follows:

TIM	Patrick J. Adams
MALLORY	Troian Bellisario
SERGEI	Alex Mickiewicz
GALINA	Natalia Payne

The Last Match was subsequently produced by City Theatre in Pittsburgh, Pennsylvania (Tracy Brigden, Artistic Director) on April 9, 2016. The director was Tracy Brigden, the stage manager Patti Kelly, the scenic designer Narelle Sissons, the costume designer Susan Tsu, the lighting designer Ann Wrightson and the sound designer Joe Pino. The cast was as follows:

TIM	Danny Binstock
MALLORY	Daina Michelle Griffith
SERGEI	JD Taylor
GALINA	Robin Abramson

When I want something– that to me is not youth exactly, but the opposite of death. That to me is a way to always feel like I am nowhere near the end.

Heidi Julavits, *The Folded Clock*

Let me put it another way: when I am with my son I feel the bracing speed of the one- way journey that guides human experience.

Sarah Manguso, *Ongoingness*

The slow-motion euthanasia that time inflicts on athletic talent is, for me, the hardest thing to watch in sports. But time is treating Federer with a tenderness that almost defies reason.

Brian Phillips, "The Sun Never Sets:
On Roger Federer, Endings and Wimbledon"

The long day wanes; the slow moon climbs; the deep
Moans round with many voices. Come, my friends,
'Tis not too late to seek a newer world.
Push off, and sitting well in order smite
The sounding furrows; for my purpose holds
To sail beyond the sunset, and the baths
Of all the western stars, until I die.
It may be that the gulfs will wash us down;
It may be we shall touch the Happy Isles,
And see the great Achilles, whom we knew.
Though much is taken, much abides; and though
We are not now that strength which in old days
Moved earth and heaven, that which we are, we are,
One equal temper of heroic hearts,
Made weak by time and fate, but strong in will
To strive, to seek, to find, and not to yield.

Tennyson, *Ulysses*

Lights up on SERGEI and TIM, who face the audience. TIM is mid-30s, wholesome, Midwestern; SERGEI is in his mid-20s and speaks with a thick Russian accent. They're both professional tennis players at the top of the game, no better athletes out there. There is also a scoreboard that keeps track of the progression of the match over the course of the play. The feeling, at the top, is of a post-match interview.

We begin at love all.

TIM: It's not exactly a whizzing sound—

SERGEI: No, it's more of a whoosh. Like a "whoosh" right past your ear—

TIM: I'd say it's fast and it's slow all at once.

SERGEI: Yeah, it's "sh-sh-sh-sh-sh" – and you are forgetting for a second that everyone is there and it's just FUCK. You think "Sergei, you asshole." You don't understand why you are not good enough.

TIM: No. For me, it was always, you know, credit to him for getting it past me.

SERGEI: *(Rolling his eyes, sarcastic.)* Oh yes, for me too. Absolutely. Credit to him.

TIM: And when *you* hit one, I mean, when you hit an ace yourself, you are…well, you are intensely *alive* in that moment.

SERGEI: From the very first point, the match was close.

TIM: In those kinds of matches, there is tension all the way through.

SERGEI: It never breaks. You are tired just from that, even more than from the physical exertions.

TIM: It had rained and now there was this eerie light when we came out on court.

SERGEI: A late start. All day I sat and then stood and then sat and then stood, shaking out my legs. That's what you do. You try to rest without staying still.

TIM: The press in New York was…the media was into it.

SERGEI: It had been leaked—Tim Porter will retire after this U.S. Open.

> What did I think? I don't know. This is sport. You play your game. It does not matter what people say.

TIM: Really, Sergei?

SERGEI: Hey, for all I know, you leaked this rumor yourself. To get in my head so I do not give my all in first ever U.S. Open semifinal. Like announcing you will die but really wanting to live and taking a very Russian-like manipulating approach to staying alive.

TIM: I didn't leak the rumor because it wasn't true.

SERGEI: Yes, that is the thing…Even with his up and down playing, even though he is old OLD man at thirty-three years of age, he is still Tim Porter, the favorite in any match he plays. You cannot imagine he will ever go away.

TIM: It's the U.S. Open. I've played it twelve times. Made ten semifinals. Nine finals. Won six of'em.

SERGEI: *(Sarcastic.)* And I have ten fingers and ten toes. I keep track of things very carefully too.

TIM: I was *gonna* say if you'd told me when I was a kid that I'd hold that trophy over my head six times, I'd have said you were the biggest liar there was.

SERGEI: But this year, how many trophies have you won?

> *TIM shoots him a dirty look.*

> Lose in Australia, second round, lose in France, quarterfinals. Wimbledon—what a loss! First round, to a qualifier, an eighteen year old from Galveston, Texas whose life will never be as good as it was that night. Yes, in last year, it has been lose lose lose.

TIM: *(With a smile, ribbing him.)* And yet… I'm still ranked in the top five and you have yet to crack the top ten, even though as a junior you were being heralded as the second coming of Christ…or of me, or something.

SERGEI: And so people talk. He must be done for, they say. The end of Tim Porter…And they want that. And also they don't want it at all.

TIM: We start the warm up.

SERGEI: Already I am hot hot hot. Like burning up hot. I can feel every tingle in every tingly spot in my body.

TIM: This is Sergei for you. Really no more than a boy.

SERGEI: No, Tim Porter, I have not felt like boy since I was five-years-old child.

TIM: Whatever you say.

SERGEI: See, we are always a little on edge with each other. Me and Tim Porter.
Not really friends.

TIM: We practice our serves. Throw the ball up, slam the racquet down. It's a motion I could do in my sleep.

SERGEI: Why don't you take it easy, Tim? You're not young anymore.

TIM: Goad all you want. I've made it through five rounds without dropping a set.

SERGEI: So have I.

TIM: This is my tournament—my house. I own this court; I always have and I will again. I have to. I have to…because my son is here. He's two months old. And it feels like the sky's a different color than it's ever been before.

SERGEI: Tim is very sentimental about this little boy.

TIM: It's the first time I've played with him in the stands. And I don't want it to be the last. After a long line of – "this has Tim's last final written all over it;" and "we might never see Tim this deep in the second week of a slam again" – it changes here. It has to. No more losing.

SERGEI: *(Getting really worked up by the end.)* No more walking off court embarrassed to be seen by anyone, especially the people you love. No more hatred for all the players ahead of you, who create such jealousy in you that you are ashamed to know yourself. To shake their hands in front of the cameras, to make nice, to smile, when really you are wishing so many bad things happen to them.

TIM: And we're only in the warm up.

SERGEI: *(An aside, to the audience.)* And yet. In the "he is done for," in the "this is the end of Tim Porter," is the end of all of us, yes?

TIM: I hate to break it to you, Sergeyev, but I'm not going anywhere.

SERGEI: I hate to break it to *you*, Tim Porter, but we're all going to the same place.

TIM: We starting, or what??

SERGEI: Yeah. I want to start.
I'm ready for you. Tim Porter.

TIM: Are you sure?

A scoreboard lights up: Set # 1.

SERGEI: He got the toss and elected to serve.

TIM: You choose to serve first no matter what. It's a psychological thing. Right, Sergei?

SERGEI: They are chanting his name: "Porter, Porter, Porter," and he wins first game pretty easily.

TIM: Yes!!

> SERGEI: *Or another way of looking at it is I lose first game pretty easily.*
>
> *Scoreboard: T. Porter, 1-0.*

TIM: I take the first game so fast and in that moment you don't feel the pressure and the failure and the death and the ambition and the coming up short. It's one of those. When you feel like you can do anything. Like you're eighteen years old, with everything in front of you.

MALLORY enters; they are mid-conversation.

MALLORY: *(Teasing him.)* You wish you were eighteen.

TIM: This is three years ago.

MALLORY: You wish you were eighteen and that your body didn't make creaking noises and that people weren't calling you old on TV.

TIM: This is Mallory.

MALLORY: But, you know, happy birthday.

TIM: Gosh, thanks honey.

MALLORY: The good thing is: I will love you even when you're actually old. And when no one talks about you on TV anymore. When they can't even remember your name.

TIM: Where's my present?

MALLORY: What present?

TIM: What do you mean "what present"?

MALLORY: Isn't it enough that all the guys on tour are celebrating today? There are parties happening all over the world. *Tim Porter turns thirty.* He's gotta start showing his age soon.

TIM: *(Playfully.)* Gimme my present. I want it.

MALLORY: I mean, I know you've been, like, winning slams and stuff, but I've been pretty busy lately too.

TIM: You know, I hope Angie knows how lucky she is. That girl won the fucking lottery with you. You were an amazing player and you're gonna be an amazing coach.

MALLORY: *(Laughing.)* Well, she's nineteen. At nineteen, you don't think about luck. You just *know* your life is gonna go exactly as planned.

TIM: She's gonna be the biggest star. And it's gonna be because of you.

> *Beat.*

MALLORY: So...do you remember when you proposed to me?

TIM: *(Teasing her.)* Gosh...*Do* I remember...?

MALLORY: I certainly hope you'd remember the best day of your life.

TIM: Well… a close second to winning Wimbledon for the first time–

MALLORY: *(Smiling.)* You're an asshole, you know that?

TIM: And you married me anyway. Because actually I'm kind of a catch.

Almost as big a catch as you…So there we were, sitting at that weirdo's wedding–

MALLORY: Inga's not that weird.

TIM: Okay, she's *objectively* weird, but it doesn't matter. She's up there *singing* her vows and I believe I took your hand. Really tenderly, *really* romantically. And it was incredibly damp.

MALLORY: That is a load of BS, Tim Porter, and you know it.

TIM: And then later in the night, I took you into the hallway–

MALLORY: Right next to the *bathrooms*–

TIM: I wanted it to be picturesque.

MALLORY: And you asked if I could feel it too.

TIM: Well, I didn't say it quite like that.

MALLORY: "Do you feel it too?" That's what you said. And I looked at you. And your face was so open, and so kind. And I did. Feel it. So I said, what if I do?

TIM: And I said: well–if you do–I think we should get married.

MALLORY: I was overwhelmed.

TIM: No, you were *silent* and I didn't know what to do, and suddenly heard myself saying…"can you dig it?"

MALLORY: And I said yes.

TIM: And it was all I could do not to say I told you so because you were such a pain when I first asked you out. But I realized it wasn't the right moment for that sorta thing. Not the right note for that particular melody.

MALLORY: Happy birthday, Timmy.

She hands him a wrapped gift.

TIM: See, I knew you got me something.

He opens the gift and pulls out a pair of plain white socks.

MALLORY: You don't like them?

TIM: *(Lying, and not very well.)* No. I love them. Thank you, honey.

She starts to walk away, but then turns back.

MALLORY: *(Totally offhand.)* Oh, and we're having a baby.

TIM: What?

MALLORY: *(Now living the emotion of it.)* We're having a baby.

TIM: *(To the audience.)* It's the most beautiful melody in the world. And for that moment you don't feel the pressure and the failure and the death and the ambition and the coming up short.

MALLORY: *(A bit teary.)* Can *you* dig it?

TIM: I can dig it.

(He takes her in his arms and kisses her. Then she exits.)

TIM: *(To the audience, sadly.)* That was the first pregnancy.

SERGEI: We're between games. We switch sides of the court. I pass Tim and even though he has won first game he looks as though he has lost it. I wonder if he is trying to "psych" me out, but I will not let him.

TIM: Then a woman in the crowd calls out–

SERGEI: This idiot camel just screams out: "We love you, Tim Porter!!" And I must tune this out. Tune it out, Sergei. You don't need their love. But the camel keeps yelling: "Don't go, Timmy, please don't go!"

TIM: Go where? I wanna say. Outside of here what would I do everyday? Would I even exist? Who would I be?

SERGEI: Oh don't worry. You'd be same gigantic asshole. Trust me.

TIM: I'm not an asshole.

SERGEI: You don't want people to *know* you're an asshole. But anyone who does this sport at this level is gigantic asshole of worst gigantic asshole variety.

TIM: I net an easy return.

SERGEI: You have to care only for yourself.

TIM: I barely manage a lob and then it lands long anyway.

SERGEI: You cannot have anything but want.

TIM: Sergei slams a volley into my face and it's all I can do to get my racquet up to protect myself.

SERGEI: I take my time. Sometimes, even though the ball is moving at such incredible speeds, you can take your time. And I did.

TIM: Three points played, three points lost. Fuck me.

SERGEI: And then I get a little confident, just a little, and I run to the net and boom—he passes me.

TIM: I'm not an asshole.

SERGEI: One shot here—another point.

TIM: I care about my family.

SERGEI: One shot there—another point.

TIM: I love my son. All my want is want for him.

SERGEI: Really, Tim Porter? *All* your want?

TIM: And suddenly it's deuce.

SERGEI: And then it is deuce again. And again. And again.

TIM: *Fourteen* deuces. Fourteen.

SERGEI: On and on and on. And the voice in my ear that is saying "take this. Just take it. It is yours. Fuck you" turns into my darling Galina's voice. Her actual voice:

GALINA: *(Like the volume's been cranked up as loud as it can go.)* TAKE IT SERGEI!! TAKE IT NOW!

SERGEI: And I know I will be in deep trouble if I do not hold this game—even more trouble than I will be in with myself.

But I can't help it—in most important matches the thought that...*I cannot win*...won't go away.

> *GALINA enters.*

GALINA: No, Sergei—when you start to think you undo yourself. Thinking is not your strength. Hitting a ball over a net at great speeds and with impressive precision—that is your strength.

SERGEI: *(With a smile, pride.)* Galina—she does not mince the words.

GALINA: Why should I not say what I mean? Why talk if you do not get your point across? Furthermore, this Tim Porter – he is beaten down. He is a little little man right now. His heart will not be in it, and you will capitalize.

SERGEI: And I say to her: his heart does not need to be in it as long as his racquet is. And she screams at me. It is right before the match and Galina and I are fighting. Okay yes. We are always fighting. So this was like always.

GALINA: No, you idiot! Don't let up on him. Not even once. Don't let him get under your skin. Once you do that, you're finished.

SERGEI: He is already under my skin—he was number one player for three years running! He is legend. His name is written on the fucking sky.

GALINA: Well, you will be legend. You will be one soon enough. If you do your job.

SERGEI: Why don't you go out there and play him if you're sure it's so simple.

GALINA: Oh, you sound like my mother: "why don't you go to work and earn the money if you insist on buying that fancy lipstick. No girl your age needs lipstick, let alone a fancy one like that, plus it make you look like whore." So I said "my lips are my lips, to do with as I please" and she said "I made those lips" and I said "I am not inside of you and have not been inside of you for many years during which time I have come to see how everything about you is despicable" and she said "you are awful terrible child, I don't believe I *did* make you" and then she retreat into her little hole where she always went instead of going to work and earning money and we did not speak for weeks and eventually I grew up, moved out of the house and found you who will go be brave in ways she could not.

SERGEI: So in other words there is no pressure on me.

GALINA: Sergei!

SERGEI: Galina!

GALINA: I am not joking around.

SERGEI: No, you never are.

GALINA: When I met you, I knew, right away, that you were a champion.

SERGEI: Did you.

GALINA: I said to Natasha "this one will make something of himself. I know it because there are things he prefers to do than spend time with me." See, in the past, my many boyfriends always put me first, above all other things. But not you. And I was so happy.

TIM: The fifteenth deuce. And the crowd is going bananas. You just want to please them, your parents times fucking a million.

SERGEI: No, the crowd is not my parents. My parents are my parents...

I wish they were here.

GALINA: Don't think of that now.
I'm here.

SERGEI: I know, but.

GALINA: Don't be scared to win. To beat him!

SERGEI: I'm not.

GALINA: You are. He is too big. This icon of your growing up. You have put an impossible pressure on yourself and it frightens you.

SERGEI: I'm not scared!!

GALINA: *(Smiling, mission accomplished; and giving him a little pat on the behind.)* Okay, okay.

SERGEI: *(Back to the audience.)* Yes, I was. I was very scared.

TIM: By this point in the game, I could really feel the whole stadium just pulling for me.

SERGEI: I try to focus on the fans. And they are really pulling for me. There are not so many Russians here but the good thing about Russians is that they are very loud.

TIM: The next day, the journalists wrote about that moment, when the crowd got to their feet. When all I could think was: "Remember this, Tim. Remember this."

SERGEI: It had never happened before like this for me. As though you are sun and everyone else is planets and stars and moons. It is, as they say, *intoxicating*, as though you have taken very strong drug like crack or cocaine, which I have only tried on handful of occasions so I cannot really comment.

TIM: I had the advantage more at the beginning but he always got out from under me. Then, somewhere in the middle, he starts winning the deuce points and I start having to grind it out.

SERGEI: So many game points, on my racquet. This should be MY game so many times over. I have earned it! But life does not actually work that way. You actually have to win.

TIM: And that's when the rumor comes back into my mind. My retirement...My retirement. And the idea of that moves through me like a wave.

SERGEI: He hits a second serve return into the net, straight into the net, and so I take it. After all those deuces, I win the game. Second game of match but it feels like I have won whole thing. Wham bam thank you, ma'am! Sergei takes it.

GALINA: Oh yes he does!

TIM: *(A stupid question.)* Was it demoralizing?

SERGEI: Galina was in my box, just going crazy. Just yelling yelling yelling. She is happy but still looks as though she might kill someone. And that is Galina at her most contained.

TIM: Yeah. It was demoralizing.

> *Scoreboard: 1-1.*

> *The lights shift. MALLORY is exercising to a video – rigorous and fast-paced. She's pushing herself incredibly hard. She's entirely focused. TIM is watching but she doesn't know he's there; then suddenly she sees him out of the corner of her eye and jumps.*

MALLORY: Jesus, how long have you been standing there?

TIM: Don't stop on my account.

> *(She turns off the video)*

MALLORY: Don't watch me, Tim. It's creepy.

TIM: Sorry…

I thought you looked good…

MALLORY: *(With a wry smile.)* Then you might need to get your eyes checked.

TIM: You were going pretty hard there.

MALLORY: *(Pumped up; this is the solution she's been looking for.)* I just started thinking maybe I shouldn't be making Angie do things I can't do myself, you know?

TIM: Oh yeah?

MALLORY: So from now on I'm gonna just show her how it's done. No more excuses. I can't stand her whining.

TIM: All right.

MALLORY: What?

TIM: It's just that I thought half the fun of coaching was *not* having to do that stuff. Not having to stay in that kind of shape.

MALLORY: Coaching isn't supposed to be fun. It's a job.

TIM: No, I just meant–

MALLORY: If I don't kill her first, that is. Do you know what she said to me today? She was like, "yeah, I heard that after thirty-five, a woman's chances of having a healthy baby go WAY down." I wanted to slap her.

TIM: Maybe you should have.

MALLORY: Right?! I mean a nineteen-year-old has no concept of–

TIM: You don't have to work with her anymore…I mean, you don't have to work at all.

She shoots him a look.

MALLORY: You know that I can't just be Tim Porter's wife.

TIM: Yeah it's hard to imagine a fate more dreadful.

MALLORY: The vessel that carried Tim Porter's children. What was her name again?

TIM: Mal. Come on.

MALLORY: The first time I sat in the stands to watch you, I came home to find stuff online about Tim Porter's /"sweaty new girlfriend."

TIM: *(With a smile, ribbing her.)* / Sweaty new girlfriend.

MALLORY: I mean, *I'd just played a match*! A second round match in the *French Open.* And won by the way. But still there I was, just a sweaty girlfriend.

TIM: Not to me.

MALLORY: I mean, what if having a baby is just boring?

TIM: Okay we're talking about babies now??

MALLORY: And some people don't even love their babies right away so it's just relentless and boring. And we already have tennis for that, right?

TIM: Well, I don't find tennis boring.

MALLORY: I know. It's shocking.

TIM: Mallory.

MALLORY: Being a father would distract you.

TIM: I'm not gonna play forever.

MALLORY: But deep inside you really think you will.

TIM: No I don't.

MALLORY: I did.

I mean, there's *still* some part of me that thinks I'll go back one day. That I'm not really done.

TIM: Don't you want to be done?

MALLORY: *(Matter-of-fact.)* Well, I always completely hated it.

TIM: You did.

MALLORY: But I miss it more than you could believe.

TIM: You miss knowing every day how deeply you're fucking over your body?

MALLORY: Knowing every day why you're in the world. In some ways it didn't even matter that I was a failure.

TIM: You weren't a failure.

MALLORY: *You* can't say that to me, honey.

TIM: You were one of the top twenty players in the whole world.

MALLORY: Uh huh. And would that have been good enough for *you*?

Beat.

Exactly. So I can't fail now. I'm gonna make her a star. Angie.

With a wry smile.

Even if she is an asshole.

TIM: …You know you haven't let me down, right? Is that what this is about?

Beat.

MALLORY: I'd be nearly six months pregnant now. Have you thought about that?

TIM doesn't say anything.

Because I think about it every day.

TIM: I know you do.

MALLORY: Not to sound…but how could you know that? I barely ever see you.

TIM: *(Back to the audience.)* Yeah, it was really fucking demoralizing. And then I'm just, I don't know, one game after the next, and I can hardly keep track of'em. They're seeping out, like milk gushing out of the carton onto the kitchen floor.

SERGEI: It is 5-1 and I am serving for the set. This is not what anyone predicted. Not even Galina predicted this. She thought I'd be fighting my tooth and my nail for every point, the whole way through.

TIM: So yeah. I lose the game, and I lose the first set.

GALINA: Yes!!

SERGEI: If I were text message, I would be exclamation point exclamation point question mark exclamation point emoticon of face of an obese sixty-year-old man who has been very badly backed up for days and has just taken biggest shit of his life.

TIM: I gave it away.

> *First set Sergeyev 6-1. They both sit for the short break between sets, SERGEI excited and jittery and TIM dejected, their body language in stark contrast. TIM covers his face with a towel and SERGEI does a quick stretch in his chair. He can't stop moving. He's amped up. Set number 2. They stand.*

SERGEI: I have all the momentum going into the second set. This is good thing, yes, but you can't get too cozy-cozy. You always must play as if you are the one behind.

TIM: My dad once said to me, "you love it, right?" meaning tennis and I was like yeah, sure, of course I love it. What do you mean, do I love it?

> *Scoreboard: Set #1, S. Sergeyev 6-1; Set # 2, 0-0.*

SERGEI: At start of second set, Tim is concentrating less and less. It is like he has decided he will lose and is simply watching it happen. I go up 1-love.

TIM: But over the years, yeah...I guess I started wondering if, really, I was just good at it, you know?

SERGEI: 2-love. And the life has gone out of the crowd. You don't want to watch a man get slaughtered so you call your wife; you get hot dog; you check stock market on your cell phone—"oh jeez, my stock is down."

TIM: A few years back, my dad had a minor thing. A minor heart attack, I guess, so not such a big deal, but...

SERGEI: Everything is going my way; I see ball so clearly, as though it is huge, like melon, and also a part of me, my hand, my fingers...

TIM: He doesn't come to my matches anymore. Made him too tense and the doctors didn't like it. But now I look up at my box and my dad isn't there. My dad...who for years ran five miles before breakfast but now wears hearing aids and gets winded walking the dog around the block. He drove me home after tennis every day of my life. We didn't really talk. He'd play his music. It was cheesy as hell and I'd complain but I think we knew we were sitting very deep in the heart of happiness. Back then.

Bang! A ball off SERGEI's racket hits TIM in the face.

SERGEI: And then I hit him in the face. He is at net and it is not my intention but in the third game of second set, this is what happens.

TIM: He hits me.

SERGEI: / And.

TIM: And I let out this totally—

SERGEI: This loud lady shriek, a scream—

TIM: *(Screaming at SERGEI.)* What the fuck was that??

SERGEI: I put up my hand in the universal gesture of apology.

TIM: That can't be sincere.

SERGEI: He says:

TIM: You're just gonna stand there?

SERGEI: So I say "what, you'd prefer I sit?" And the crowd laughs.

> *(GALINA is cracking up.)*

TIM: That's it. For the past two years, when I've lost more than I've won, at least, at the very least, the crowd has been with me. And my *son* is here. My son is here today...So this was...

SERGEI: He goes crazy.

TIM: *(A humble admission.)* I go a little nuts.

MALLORY: Settle down, Tim. It doesn't matter. Just settle down!

SERGEI: He goes cuckoo. Which for me would be just normal changeover between games, but for Tim is very out of character. Very out of the carefully sculpted character he has built all these years. Not a hair out of place.

TIM: *(Angry and awkwardly delivered.)* I never really liked you— no offense.

SERGEI: No that is not offensive in the least.

TIM: I don't like players like you. Your antics and tantrums and fancy shot-making. I mean, what does it amount to? You've been underperforming your entire career.

SERGEI: I couldn't agree more.

TIM: I mean, who do you think you are??

SERGEI: I am just Sergei Sergeyev, a poor boy from tiny fishing village on Caspian Sea.

TIM: Oh come on. Don't play that humble beginnings crap with me!

SERGEI: But is true. I did not grow up in Iowa with silver spoon where my dick should be.

TIM: And now you're doing just fine for yourself I'd say. I bet you bought your parents a Porsche last week.

MALLORY: Tim! That's enough.

SERGEI: Actually I gave your mother brand new Porsche after two times fucking her in backseat.

GALINA: *(Watching, her head in her hands.)* Oh, Sergei.

TIM: He really said that. And then Drobek, in the chair, is like "cool it" and Sergei is docked a point.

SERGEI: Me?? *I* am docked the point? It's un-fucking-believable. I mean, yes, I did hit him so hard in face with tennis ball that there is for days afterwards a mark on upper part of his left cheek but that is not against the rules.

TIM: Just because something isn't against the rules doesn't mean you do it!

SERGEI: But I didn't mean to do it!

TIM: You're the best fucking tennis player in the world, don't tell me you didn't mean to do it!

> *A breath.*

SERGEI: *(With real surprise and humility.)* You think I'm the best fucking tennis player in the world?

TIM: You are.

> *Scoreboard: Set #2 S. Sergeyev 2-0*

> *SERGEI is humbled. GALINA enters the scene, seamlessly.*

GALINA: *(To an unseen waiter.)* Waiter? Waiter, do you know who this is?

SERGEI: *(He actually loves this.)* Stop it, Galina. You embarrass me.

GALINA: This man will one day be the best tennis player in the entire world. You should pay him the respect of bringing us some water and some bread within our first twenty minutes of sitting in your supposedly fine establishment, which, might I add, could use a little sprucing up. You are only *two* star Michelin restaurant for a reason, I think. Also. I would like to revise my order. Instead I will have the flounder but without the potatoes and without the buerre blanc and without any garnish of any kind. I detest garnish of any kind.

SERGEI: So that is basically just piece of fish. That is all you want?

GALINA: No, I want everything in the world, but I also know what I am and am not capable of. I know that if I eat a pizza pie, I will want another pizza pie. I know if I start down a road I will stay on it.

SERGEI: Compulsive? I am this way too, of course.

GALINA: Did you know I was once two hundred pounds, in my childhood?

SERGEI: You were not.

GALINA: I was not. But I felt like I was. Like no one would ever really see me. My mother, she perpetuated this myth and then it became the myth by which I live my life. We all have them, these myths. These fictions, but still they control who we are.

What is yours?

SERGEI: My what?

GALINA: Your myth?

SERGEI: *(Deflecting her question.)* I do not live by myth.

GALINA: You are disagreeing with me?

SERGEI: *(Seeing the error of his ways.)* No. No I am not. I must have myth.

GALINA: What is the thing you want most in the world?...I for example want to be taken seriously for who I am and not for my body.

SERGEI: Then why do you care so much about your body?

GALINA: Would you be with me if not for my body?

(Beat.)

SERGEI: No.

GALINA: So I am realistic. I need it to get the things I want. After all, one day you will take me seriously. When you get to know me.

SERGEI: Oh don't worry—I already take you seriously.

GALINA: I was surprised, you know. Your trainer Uly told my cousin Maria that you were a handful. That you had these rages. That you could not be controlled. And then I meet you and you are just this little mouse.

SERGEI: That is because you terrify me.

GALINA: It's true—we are so many different people. This is why I act. It merely emphasizes what is already the case.

SERGEI: You did the commercial for that...plant fertilizer? Uly shows me this on the YouTube. It's funny—that was a wig, yes?

GALINA: I was paid well for that.

SERGEI: So what other parts have you played?

GALINA: Are you making a cross-examination of me, Sergei?

SERGEI: No, I am trying to understand if you are real actor or if it is just dream hobby of yours.

GALINA: How would you like it if I asked if you were real tennis player? What kind of question is this?

SERGEI: I am clearly a real tennis player because I play tennis. All the time.

GALINA: Well, I cannot act whenever I want to—I must be chosen! And this is indignity I do not enjoy and so I do not put myself in the position of facing it very often.

SERGEI: So you are scared.

GALINA: *(Standing to leave.)* Okay. I curse you, and I am leaving because as it turns out you are not at all the kind of person I could ever like or be with!

SERGEI: *(Stopping her from walking out.)* Let me tell you something: right now I am number fourteen player in the world, yes?

GALINA: So what?

SERGEI: When I went pro, I thought it would be something if one day I could crack top twenty. I thought: that is all I need to be happy in this life.

GALINA: Well, congratulations. You did it.

SERGEI: But that is the thing—I'm not happy. I have to crack top ten. And when I do, I will need to be better than that. It will go on forever. Even when I am the best fucking tennis player in the world. I am sure of it.

TIM: When I first got number one, I thought: *yes*. I mean, you can't really take it in. *Number one*, right? Fuuuuuck…But the next morning was a gut punch. I woke up sweating, just thinking: how long can I stay here? How can I possibly stay here?

SERGEI: Will you please sit back down.

GALINA: Why?

SERGEI: Because I love you and I want to have dinner with you and have a nice night and to do that you have to sit back down.

> *A beat.*

GALINA: Oh you love me, do you?

SERGEI: *(Smiling bashfully.)* …Yeah.

GALINA: Ah. So this is your myth. That love can triumph in the end.

SERGEI: Galina, I am Russian. I do not believe in triumph of love. But I do believe it is possible to have nice meal now and then. Is that too much to ask?

GALINA: For people like us, it might be almost too much to ask.

SERGEI: I bet Tim Porter has nice meal with his wife every single night!

GALINA: But Tim Porter's worst nightmare is probably getting speeding ticket. He was not raised as we were raised. So aware of death.

SERGEI: Okay, this is not conversation that is going to lead to enjoying our meal.

GALINA: Sergei, do you ever feel like, when you are playing tennis in front of all those people, everything else—who you are, what you like, what you fear—drops away? I like to think it feels this way, to play. I cannot have that, but I hope you can. You can escape your own death.

SERGEI: Why do you think I am afraid of my own death?

GALINA: Everyone is afraid of this. My mother in particular, maybe. And also me.

He looks at her, and takes her hand.

SERGEI: Yes: it is very nice when everything else drops away.

TIM: When did we first meet, Sergei?

SERGEI: So I am docked point for claiming to fuck Tim Porter's mother in backseat of car.
And Tim is fired up. And he takes that game.
And he takes the next two games. So he is now up 3-2 in the second set.

TIM: When did we meet?

SERGEI: You are trying to distract me. I'm returning your serve. I'm behind in set. Don't distract me.

TIM: The locker-room at Indianapolis?

SERGEI: *(Suddenly exploding.)* The locker-room at Indianapolis?? Really?? Really??

To the audience, an aside.

Of course I remember exactly when I met Tim Porter. It was not in locker-room at Indianapolis.

TIM: It was in Atlanta. I'd been hearing about this guy, Sergei Sergeyev. He wasn't going deep in tournaments but he was supposedly this well of untapped potential. Once he could release it, he'd be great. So I watched him play. And it was fascinating – you could literally see every thought *as he was having it* – he couldn't hide a thing. Did he play well? No, not in slightest…but I couldn't stop thinking about him, about what it would feel like not to wear any armor.

SERGEI: After my match, we run into Tim. Which is…I mean, *this* is when I meet Tim Porter?? After I embarrass myself so terribly on court? But my coach introduces us. He says, mark his words, I am going to be next Tim Porter. And Tim says:

TIM: *(Sarcastic.)* Good luck with that, Sergei.

SERGEI: As though being Tim Porter is so unpleasant it is not something to which one should aspire. Which surprises me. That Tim Porter should seem more unhappy than me, even though I am the one who just got miserably beaten by player with no skill, and no style, and no business being out on tennis court.

TIM: Why don't you say what you really feel.

SERGEI: I think you knew where we met. You were just trying to distract me. And it's not gonna work.

TIM: Yes it will. And I pass him down the line – this thing of beauty – and I take the game. 4-2.

SERGEI: No no no no no no no no. Shit. Fuck. Balls.

TIM: He throws his racquet. He jams that thing into the ground and tosses it aside. And then like an animal, he tears his shirt off. Literally, rips it off. This is not a good thing. The truth is…when Sergei gets angry, he gets good, and he knows this as well as anyone.

GALINA: *(With satisfied calm; she knows this is good.)* It is okay to get angry, Sergei. You do what you need to do.

TIM: He takes his service game easily—just so *easily*. I net two returns, completely eff up an overhead, just—"whiff"—it's over my head. I mistimed it.

SERGEI: I ace him. And I won't lie. It's like sex. The best angry-I-will-not-forgive-you sex you have ever had.

TIM: It's an exclamation point. That's what an ace is. And depending on the mood, it's a "fuck you exclamation point."

SERGEI: This was a "fuck you" ace.

GALINA: Yes!

TIM: *(To the audience.)* But I can match him. I go there too. The adrenaline kicks in, zero to sixty.

Scoreboard: Set # 2, T. Porter 4-3.

SERGEI: Tim serves at 4-3. He answers with two aces—what a motherfucking camel—and then a serve and volley winner for forty love. Then the call happens. He foot faults.

TIM: "A FOOT FAULT?"

SERGEI: He contests the call.

TIM: You've gotta be kidding me!

SERGEI: It is, admittedly, a bad call, but of course it is not my place to intervene.

TIM: You can't call a *foot fault* in the semifinals of the U.S. goddamn Open!!"

MALLORY: Calm down, Tim. You have to calm down!

TIM: *(TIM's awkward at insults.)* And I never foot fault! I never do it. I tell the line umpire: engage in a sexual act with your own mother!

MALLORY: What's come over you, Timmy?? Who are you tonight??

SERGEI: He loses point and then he loses game. And then he loses next game, so I am up 5-4.

GALINA: You can do it, Sergei. You've got it all— younger legs, stronger serve, longer arms, quicker feet. You are like a bird flying light on the wind compared to him.

SERGEI: And then I am up 40-15 and serving for the second set. Win *one* point and I am up two sets! The match is going according to plan, which is something, really something! But just as I am congratulating myself, I catch glimpse of Tim's box—of his mother holding that little baby and his so anxious wife, and when I look in my box, my parents are not there and I have no children and no brothers or sisters and Galina will be my wife one day but she is not always so nice to me and I know this, I know it, and so I must be playing only for myself and I am not sure, in that moment, if that is enough…And I lose the game.

TIM: *(Pumping himself up.)* Come on!!

Come on.

You got this, Tim. You can do it.

> *The lights shift. TIM looks at MALLORY, who sits on a bench, on a practice court, her racquet on her lap. He goes to sit down beside her. He's as smooth as can be.*

TIM: Stacy, right?

MALLORY: What?

TIM: That's your name—Stacy, am I right?

MALLORY: Um. No.

TIM: Shit. Really?

Well, what is it?

MALLORY: We've, um, we've met before.

TIM: Is that right?

MALLORY: We were juniors…

TIM: No. When?

MALLORY: I'm not gonna tell you that.

TIM: Oh, come on. Throw me a bone.

> *(She doesn't say anything.)*

Was it at Bollettieri?

MALLORY: I never trained there.

TIM: In Palm Springs?

MALLORY: You really don't remember?

TIM: I meet so many people. You have to forgive me. My brain is just…

MALLORY: *(With a smile, teasing him.)* It's hard to be you, isn't it.

TIM: Come on, be nice.

MALLORY: *(Teasing.)* Okay. I'm sorry. I'm sorry you win every match you play.

TIM: I nearly lost today.

MALLORY: *(Laughing drily.)* Can I ask you…

TIM: What?

MALLORY: When someone comes that close, is there any part of you that wants to give it to them? Like they deserve it for even getting *close* to beating you?

TIM: Never. You always have to feel like it's yours and they're trying to take it from you. I honestly wouldn't even get on court if I felt there was a chance I was gonna lose.

MALLORY: Wow.

TIM: What?

MALLORY: Maybe you could lend me a little of that? I promise to give it back.

TIM: You've got a match today, don't you?

MALLORY: *(Surprised that he knows this.)* Yeah.

TIM: Petrokova's good. She's got great court coverage. But you'll be fine. Just don't be afraid to exploit her weaknesses. Her forehand return of serve is crappy so hit it there every time. And don't be nervous.

MALLORY: Did I say I was nervous?

TIM: …Do you know what *your* weakness is?

MALLORY: *(Bold, flirty.)* Oh, you know *my* weakness too?

TIM: It's also your strength…

MALLORY: And what's that?

TIM: You anticipate balls so well because you're inside the mind of your opponent. But you're in it too deep. And you start to feel for them.

> *Beat.*

It's a wonderful quality in a person.

MALLORY: *(With a wry smile.)* Maybe not in a tennis player though.

TIM: But who cares about that.

MALLORY: You really don't remember meeting me?

TIM: Wait a second.

MALLORY: What.

TIM: Was it...Rhode Island?

> *She doesn't say anything.*

You won that award?

MALLORY: Which award?

TIM: Was it...Sportsmanship?

MALLORY: I am a very good sport.

TIM: You were that night, with me rambling on and on.

MALLORY: So you do remember.

TIM: Talk about nervous.

MALLORY: Why were you nervous?

TIM: Sitting next to YOU?

MALLORY: Come on, I was sitting next to YOU. And even at 16, you were already...

TIM: You were the famous one! The gal who gives out hugs after every match.

MALLORY: I don't understand how anyone *doesn't* do that. You've just been through so much together.

TIM: And there I was thinking a match was about going through so much on your own.

MALLORY: It makes me less nervous to think of it like you're both putting on this show, together.

TIM: Are you nervous right now?

MALLORY: About my match?

TIM: No.

MALLORY: No, I'm not nervous.

TIM: Well I am.

MALLORY: Why?

TIM: Cuz I'm finally gonna get up the nerve to ask you out.

Beat.

MALLORY: Well, I hate to break it to you, but I don't date guys on tour. I don't even really talk to people on tour.

TIM: I know. It's been hard to find you. I've been trying. For, like, ten years.

MALLORY: It's not gonna happen, Tim Porter.

He turns away as if defeated, then turns back.

TIM: You know…one day we're gonna have children and we're gonna say to them "can you believe your mom said no the first time your dad asked her out?"

MALLORY: A minute ago you didn't even know my name.

TIM: I did. I do: Mallory Beth Sinclair.

She looks at him in surprise.

See? I know the whole thing.

SERGEI: He is very wily, Tim Porter. He sneaks up on you like snake. From 5-5, he holds his serve. And then I am serving once again, only now I am down 5-6.

And he passes me on the backhand side with his trademark Tim Porter forehand on a point when I should not have approached the net. He passes me on the forehand side on another point when I should not have approached the net. It is looking like clinic for kids on the passing shot. Humiliating.

And then, to make matters worse, at love-thirty, I double fault.

I double fault.

To make it triple set point. Triple break point.

All I can say is it is not fun. To be me out on court right now.

Especially when I lose the very next point, or rather Tim wins it. He hits a winner down the line because *he* is a winner. And I lose. I lose the set.

TIM: The crowd goes crazy. Just absolutely bonkers. USA, they chant. USA. "Tim Porter for President" someone cries out.

SERGEI: Because if Tim can still play, then we are all still young and *nepobedimyy* – invincible.

TIM: I can't help it. I take a bow. I know it's a jerk move, but they're applauding. They love me. How many more times will I have this?

SERGEI: At this moment I cannot stand to look at Tim Porter. Who was once, I admit it…my idol.

GALINA: Sergei, what are you doing?

> *She enters a flashback.*

SERGEI: What?

GALINA: You were falling asleep. At the table.

SERGEI: Was I?

GALINA: I guess you were not fascinated by my cautionary tale of the tennis player my second cousin Vladlena married who had so much potential but left the tour in favor of small apartment in Miami where now Vladlena runs nail salon and he is tennis pro for elderly American Jews.

SERGEI: *(To the audience.)* What I do not say to my Galina is that maybe it is better that this man should have the love of a nice woman in Miami than the dream of playing professional tennis. After all, what are dreams but distractions from something else you have lost?

GALINA: Did you hear me, Sergei? Or are you still asleep??

SERGEI: *(To the audience.)* The night before I had not slept. Maybe one hour. Maybe two. It was that kind of night where you don't know how much you are awake or asleep. This is how most nights were for me.

GALINA: What do you mean you don't get any sleep? How do you play tennis without any sleep?

SERGEI: No, I sleep. Just not great. I don't sleep great.

GALINA: For how long?

SERGEI: Forever.

GALINA: And you never tried to fix it?

SERGEI: You are not sounding sympathetic. I mean, I lie there, staring at ceiling for hours. Every day I am in little bit of hell because I know night will come and I will have to do that ordeal.

GALINA: So what do you think about. As you lie there.

SERGEI: I don't tell people this.

GALINA: We are going back to your house and you will tell me.

SERGEI: My house?

GALINA: Yes.

SERGEI: And so we went. It is difficult to say no to Galina! I had been holding her at arm's length, saying goodnight at end of dates with kiss on cheek. But I had been wanting this even at the same time as I didn't want it. You have to know that up close, Galina has eyes like stars in sky–bright and dark at once. They are unlike any other eyes I have ever seen.

GALINA: Okay, so tell me.

SERGEI: I don't know.

GALINA: *(She can be a real bully.)* Just tell me!!

SERGEI: Okay, well…When I was child, I would picture myself hitting ball after ball. And you would think the monotony of this would send one to sleep, but instead it kept me awake, with the fear that I would miss. You see I was very hard on myself. I had to be. No one – not my parents, not my friends – no one played any sport. But I displayed an extreme skill with hand and eye coordination when I was eleven months old baby and when I turned three, my father's friend Mikhael took me to a court and hit with me, and I couldn't get enough. I never wanted to leave.

GALINA: *(Prodding him to get to the point.)* But eventually you did. Because here you are.

SERGEI: At age of nine, I left home. I trained in Italy, and I trained in France, and I trained in America. Always sleeping in bunk beds, smelling other boys' feet. No home. Except for this game. And yet these days, when I cannot sleep, the game is not my home. I see myself hitting balls wildly—no control. I cannot avoid making a mistake. My parents are watching, and I am so embarrassed—I mean *this* is what I left you to do?

To play tennis *badly*?

> *He looks at her, with need in his eyes.*

GALINA: You lost your parents?

I mean…they are gone?

SERGEI: I didn't say that.

GALINA: I know.

SERGEI: They were killed in crash, almost ten years ago. They were on their way to see me play. The flight was delayed, and they called me from the airport. "We might not make it," they said. "Don't be mad."

I was fifteen-years-old.

I won that match, 7-5, 7-5.

And they weren't there.

GALINA: I am sorry, Sergei.

SERGEI: That was last match of my childhood. That was the last one.

> *Beat.*

GALINA: You know, I too have trouble falling asleep. I never just relax; it always feels there is some way I could help my situation if I could only think of it. This is true from when I was a girl. And maybe it was those long nights that finally got me on plane to America, even though I had no prospects, just cousin with sofa-bed who said Galina, come here and you can be model; you can be actress, no big deal. There is money falling out of trees if you can only catch it.

SERGEI: So what do you do to get to sleep? When you have trouble?

GALINA: As a child, since my mother was not so much around, my grandma, my babushka, she would put me to sleep. She loved me. I don't know why, but she did. And I would cling to that love like drowning girl holding onto piece of driftwood in middle of vast ocean.

SERGEI: A wonderful metaphor.

GALINA: Thank you. Especially I would cling to it at night. Because in sleep you don't know what you will face: your terrible mother or the father you never met. Or worst—you might run into yourself.

SERGEI: I would always love to run into you.

GALINA: So I would lay my head on my grandma's lap. She was sharp and bony and brittle but somehow her lap was still soft. And she'd say: close your eyes, Galina.

SERGEI's are still open.

Close your eyes.

SERGEI closes his; he is lying with his head in GALINA's lap.

She'd say: are they good and closed? No peeking. She'd say: now make sure you're in a comfortable position. Think of this position as your home for the night.

And then say to yourself—in your head, in the voice inside yourself—say "goodnight toes." And when you feel your toes go quiet, you will know that they are asleep. Once they are, say "goodnight ankles." Wait for them. Some parts of the body are more stubborn than others. Then "goodnight calves, goodnight knees." You are working your way up. "Goodnight thighs, goodnight tummy."

SERGEI: *(With his eyes closed, whispering.)* I think you missed something.

GALINA: Goodnight hands. Goodnight elbows. Goodnight chin. Goodnight nose. Goodnight eyes…Goodnight day. Goodnight body…Goodnight, Sergei. Goodnight.

> *He is asleep. Beat. The lights shift back to the match. SERGEI's eyes are still closed as he sits in his chair; TIM sits at the front of his chair, eager to get going again.*
>
> *Scoreboard: Set #1, S. Sergeyev 6-1, Set # 2, T. Porter 7-5, Set # 3, 0-0*
>
> *SERGEI finally opens his eyes. We move from silence into action.*

SERGEI: *(Quietly, from sitting.)* It is third set. And the sky is so dark and the lights so bright it seems like almost day.

TIM: The third set. The third set. And also we're starting all over again.

> *SERGEI and TIM stand, slowly.*

SERGEI: But it doesn't mean the slate is clean. There is always baggage. They say, "they are even at one set apiece," but really we are not even.

TIM: I serve first. And now it's a question of music. Of jazz. Of poetry. I mean, you know your favorite song? How sometimes you don't even notice you're singing it? It's like that.

SERGEI: From very moment we were born, we were not even. Me and Tim Porter.

TIM: It's the last thing Sergei could want. It's been written that Tim Porter in his stride is a better player than any who's ever lived. And no, it wasn't my mother who wrote that. That was the *New York Times*, I believe.

SERGEI: Oh come on—you know precisely it was *New York Times*. You probably know the date.

TIM: *(Can insert more recent date here if need be.)* August fourth, twenty-twelve. Chris Clarey.

SERGEI: There are some athletes, they say, whose powers seem more than human. Tim is one of those. In certain moments, it looks like he was born with a racquet in his hand and a purpose. Unlike the rest of us, who must choose who we are and what we do.

TIM: It's like I'm sailing, that's what it's like. And I'm up 2-love in the third set.

MALLORY: You go, Tim. You've got this.

SERGEI: I can't do anything about it. It is like I am fourteen again and watching Tim play on tiny television set in my room at the academy.

TIM: I kid you not I know exactly where each ball is gonna go *before* he even hits it. And it feels…

SERGEI: *(A genuine, searching question.)* How *does* it feel?

TIM: *(Humbled.)* It feels…like I will never die.

It feels like I am living precisely the life I was supposed to live.

SERGEI: Wow.

TIM: Yeah.

SERGEI: On the television set, he always wins. And all of the boys at the academy are in awe. If only someday we can be on center court too.

GALINA: You are on center court, Sergei! You have made it! You are here. You deserve this too! *You* are beautiful!

TIM: But it's like Sergei's just…disappeared.

SERGEI: My parents…they didn't want me to play. They thought it was too much. This life. Also they were just humble people, with a little boat. Why do you need to conquer the world? We don't care if you are something great. You are our boy and we love you.

TIM: He's getting the ball back, but his heart's not in it.

SERGEI: In this set, the third set, while I lose and lose and lose, I am twelve years old. I am home for rare visit and my father and I are out for walk at end of the day. He says to me, "Sergei, race me to that tree over there." And this is surprising because my father does not run–he does not do much that is physical activity. But I am always up for a contest so I take off and he takes off and up until this time I have never beaten my father, not at anything. But I am indeed victorious and I look back and my father is panting and there is a look on his face that is confusing to me; I don't know what to do with it so I say "race me to the next tree" and he is too much proud not to so we take off and once again I win. He is panting and holding his knees. And then I say "the next tree" and again we set off. I can't stop. I am so young and so confused and my father is slower with every tree and finally he is on the ground and he says "no more, Sergei, no more."

GALINA: *(Gently.)* Come on, Sergei, get back in the game.

SERGEI: He did not want me to beat him, and I did not want to beat him but still I did it; I don't know why.

MALLORY: Unbelievable, Timmy. You're playing like you played a decade ago.

TIM: I am in love with this set. This set is my mother, and my father when he came to my matches and I would look up at him after every point. This set…is my wife and how easy it was to love her, and it's me as a boy, feeling like I'll be in the world forever. This set has me wrapped in its embrace and it's so warm and so right and I'm playing the best tennis of my life. Of the thirty-three years of my life.

SERGEI: It is in this moment, for first time, that it occurs to me that I want to stop playing tennis.

GALINA: Seryozha, please…

SERGEI: And also that I cannot stop.

Scoreboard: Set # 3; T. Porter 5-0.

TIM: I don't feel old, not now. And it actually kinda pisses me off. How good I feel. It makes me wanna clock those numbskulls who think I'm done. I'm not done! Why would anyone stop doing this?

SERGEI: It is my whole life.

On the other hand, I do not enjoy it and it is my whole life. And life is short.

TIM: Sergei slams one at me, out of nowhere. It lands at my feet, and I pick it up; I scoop gently, the way you field a ball in baseball; I barely touch it; I'm not thinking; I'm just doing, and it's back over the net—the softest, quietest little drop shot you've ever seen.

GALINA: *(Quietly, under her breath.)* Come on, Sergei. You've got it all—younger legs, longer arms, quicker feet. You are like a bird flying light on the wind compared to him.

TIM: How could I ever let this go?

MALLORY: You did it. You did it. Holy shit you did it, Tim.

TIM: I take the set. Easiest set of my life.

> *The men take a short break.*
>
> *Scoreboard: Set # 1, S. Sergeyev 6-1; Set # 2, T. Porter 7-5; Set # 3; T. Porter 6-0.*
>
> *The fourth set. The men stand again.*

SERGEI: When we stand up to start the fourth set, there's a swell in the crowd. The stadium, it starts to rumble. It starts to move.

GALINA: *(Chanting, slowly.)* Sergei. Sergei. Sergei.

TIM: You can feel something shifting.

> *SERGEI looks up at GALINA, grateful and surprised.*

GALINA: Sergei. Sergei. Sergei.

TIM: She starts chanting his name.

MALLORY: Ignore it, Timmy.

GALINA: Who are you, Sergei? Say your name.

TIM: You've gotta be kidding me. The crowd joins in. *Sergei. Sergei.*

GALINA: Who are you Sergei??

SERGEI: They are chanting *my* name? That cannot be. I cannot be hearing right.

GALINA: Who are you, Sergei? The people, they want to know you! Let them know you!

SERGEI: Who am I? I am orphan from Kaspiysk!

GALINA: Who are you?

SERGEI: I am trapped in body of tennis player who will never get out from under his life.

GALINA: That's not true! You are living your life! This is it! This is your life! Who are you??!!

SERGEI: Sergei! I am Sergei!!!

MALLORY: It doesn't mean anything. It's just a momentary… Everyone here is here for *you*, honey!

TIM: It's my own fault. I made it look too easy. Made him too much of an underdog. And they want a match. No one wants to go home.

GALINA: You can do it, my love!!

SERGEI: I can do it! I can do it!!

TIM: It's amazing. How all of a sudden it seems like he's three times the size, covering the court like a giant.

SERGEI: I move through my service game like precision master. One shot here—oh, Tim, you are too slow. One shot there—I'm sorry, Tim, you can't get a racquet on that one.

TIM: Fuck.

SERGEI: It's fun. I am inside of it again and it's fun in there.

MALLORY: Don't let him get to you, Timmy. You're my guy. You can do it. You're our guy.

TIM: And she holds up our son like a trophy and I'm running all over the court, sliding and reaching and grasping.

SERGEI: I'm running you ragged.

TIM: She's holding our son. And I keep thinking: he won't remember this, but also he will. He'll be told. It'll be on the Internet for the rest of time for god's sake. Video of him in the stands, while his dad struggled. Which is exactly what I *wouldn't* want him to see: all of the suffering that goes along with desire.

SERGEI: Not too much left in the tank, maybe, eh?

TIM: *(To SERGEI.)* No no, I've got lots left in the tank.

>*To audience.*

And to prove it, I lunge for a drop shot. I run from behind the baseline up to the net and I lunge and—

SERGEI: And on the third point of second game of fourth set—

>*TIM goes down, in intense pain. He tries to get back up, but he can't.*

His back goes out.

TIM: *(Through gritted teeth.)* Shit!

>*We enter a flashback; we weave in and out of it.*

MALLORY: Where does it hurt?

TIM: Shit shit shit.

MALLORY: Timmy?

TIM: It's not a where; it's everywhere. It's everywhere.

MALLORY: This doesn't usually happen in the middle of the night. I mean, it just hit you, just like that? It woke you up?

SERGEI: What people don't realize is how painful it is to try to get well fast. If you are not an athlete, you just let the body heal, slow slow, on its own terms. If you are an athlete… you play through it, which of course makes it even worse.

MALLORY: Maybe we should call a doctor.

TIM: No. No doctors.

SERGEI: Tim is kneeling down. He is retching on the court, like rabid dog. And everyone just stares. It is, after all, a spectacle. And this is a spectator sport.

MALLORY: On a scale from 1-10, what is it.

TIM: I don't know. 8.

MALLORY: So it's really a 10.

>*She kneels down next to TIM, tries to still him, to knead his back, his shoulder; TIM calls out in pain.*

TIM: Aaaaah!

MALLORY: I made it worse?

TIM: Just mix me the drink. Please. Just do the drink.

> *She stands, goes to a table and takes liquids and powders out of her bag.*

MALLORY: I can do that.

But no cortisone shot because we did one a few weeks ago.

TIM: Maybe one of those too.

MALLORY: I can't stand this. I hate to see you this way.

TIM: I would be okay if you just HURRIED THE SLIGHTEST BIT. Could you go any slower, Mallory? God.

MALLORY: Please don't speak to me that way.

TIM: I'm sorry.

MALLORY: Okay.

TIM: It's just that I'm in fucking agonizing fucking pain!

> *MALLORY hands him the drink. TIM sits up and drinks it; the pain abates.*

MALLORY: You've gotta just get the surgery, Tim.

TIM: Not gonna happen.

MALLORY: I don't care if you miss a season.

TIM: Well, I do.

MALLORY: I didn't wanna get my knee fixed but I had to, and so I did it.

TIM: And then you never played again!

MALLORY: Okay, I'm gonna go back to bed.

TIM: No—you can't.

MALLORY: I don't like being screamed at in the middle of the night.

TIM: I'm sorry this isn't the most convenient time for you, but I can't exactly control when this happens!!

MALLORY: *(Cutting him off, a weapon.)* I had a miscarriage! Yesterday.

> *Beat.*

TIM: What?

MALLORY: Yesterday morning. During your match.

TIM: No you didn't.

MALLORY: I didn't tell you I was pregnant. I didn't want to. But I was.

Nine weeks.

> *Beat.*

TIM: You shoulda told me, Mal.

> *She doesn't say anything.*

You should've told me.

> *She doesn't say anything.*

My god, I don't want you going through this alone.

MALLORY: No way around that, Timmy.

TIM: Well…then maybe we should stop.

MALLORY: What?

TIM: I can't watch you…I can't let you do this to yourself.

MALLORY: Are you crazy? We can't stop now. Not after everything I've…

TIM: I don't want you doing this for me. I can't bear that.

MALLORY: Oh *you* can't bear it?

TIM: I'm sorry, I–

MALLORY: Do you want me to be a failure at everything I set out to do?

TIM: What? No.

MALLORY: It's one thing not to make the top ten in the world; it's another thing not to be able to have a child. I mean, any idiot can have a child. My *parents* could have children.

And then fuck them up by getting divorced and showing them nothing ever works.

TIM: That's not true.

MALLORY: For you, Tim. For you.

TIM: I think – understandably – everything feels awful to you at this particular moment. But…

MALLORY: If we stopped now, I would never forgive myself.

TIM: I would forgive you.

MALLORY: No. We keep going.

SERGEI: Tim takes a timeout. He leaves the court. And I wait. It is the longest three minutes of my life.

TIM: *(To the audience.)* I've always thought if a player doesn't wake up in some kinda pain, they're doing something wrong. And that's just the deal. Eleven month season. No one to sub in for you. It's brutal. You can't add to that worrying about your body ten years down the line. If you did, no one would play at all. It's not a pretty picture, what you're doing to your body.

SERGEI: I decide that when he comes back I will not show any mercy.

TIM: There is no place where you are more alone than in your own body.

SERGEI: I have had two operations. My elbow. My hip. I understand this pain, but if you are playing, I will play you, Tim Porter.

TIM: I'm numb all over from the anti-flams. And my back is taped so much I feel like a damn mummy. And because I can't feel my body I'm even more conscious of it. Of how I might look.

SERGEI: He walks back on court very slowly. And oddly tall like he has taken moment to Google "good posture."

TIM: Sometimes you need other people to let you know you're okay. And they know you need that. And they give it to you.

SERGEI: There is a roar. And the crowd, it loves him again. He is hurt and he is their golden boy so they must heal him.

TIM: The thing is, your body is *your* body, to do with what you want.

SERGEI: Like the world making room for Tim, once again. And it lifts him up.

TIM: So I'm gonna use it while I still can.

SERGEI: He takes his game. He keeps the points short and hits winner after winner.

TIM: I find some new gear. Full of shortcuts.

SERGEI: It is, frankly, embarrassing to lose to someone so clearly injured. So what do I do? I lose to him *again*. Why not, right? He breaks my serve if you can believe it.

TIM: Fuck yeah I do. I tie it right up. 2-all.

Scoreboard: Set # 4; T. Porter 2-2.

But then without meaning to I glance at my box. And Mallory's head's in her hands. She's not watching. She can't look at me.

SERGEI: Tim? Are you taking another timeout, Tim?

TIM: The thing is…when you have trouble having a baby, you walk through the world a little differently. You stare at other people's children. Sometimes you feel your throat closing up, like you can't breathe.

Your parents stop knowing what to say.

I mean, the first time we told them Mal was pregnant, my mom cried. The next day she called and said how she'd been remembering when *I* was a baby. That all these things came rushing back to her. Those nights after I was just born.

The parents are trying to be enthusiastic.

The second time, they said, "that's wonderful, you two. Truly."
The third time, they said, "oh really? Gosh. Gosh…"

SERGEI: He cannot stop looking up at box. So I look up too. And my Galina? She is glaring at me. How could I be letting this walking injury defeat me? Many years from now, I remember that look. It will be the look I will see whenever I disappoint her. Which I will do, from time to time. Because that is what happens, in life.

For instance, last year at U.S. Open, I went through three matches like they were nothing. And then in fourth round, I play Bartok who I roomed with at the academy. He has never beaten me, but when we are playing I am remembering how he cried in his sleep for his mother, and he tramples me in this match. And afterwards I am so ashamed. I am walking through the hallways in daze and I do not look up. Until someone says:

TIM: You'll get him next time, Sergei.

SERGEI: And it is Tim Porter.

TIM: Your head wasn't in it.

SERGEI: And I say "no, my head was nowhere close to that match." And he smiles and says he can count on one hand number of matches where his head stayed in match whole time. And he says my footwork is very–

TIM: You've got some really fancy footwork going there.

SERGEI: And that made me happy, that Tim Porter should take any time out of his day to consider my footwork. And then he walks away. And it occurs to me that he was condescending to me. And that adds injury to insult as you say in America. And so I get frustrated. When will my life be easy?? And that night Galina has gone to bed and I am drinking with Uly and these two ladies come up to us and they are very nice; they say how they love watching me play and I move like Canadian maple syrup what have you what have you. And I am thinking so much my life is unfair– why would Tim Porter say that about my footwork??–that when one of them puts her hand on my dick under the table–she is not shy, I guess–I let her leave it there. And when she suggests we go to her hotel room, yes I go with her. And we fuck so much. And in this time

181

I do not *think about anything*, which feels incredible, even better than the sex we are having.

TIM: Mallory still won't look at me. And now I can feel my back again. It's not a good sign when you're wishing you were still numb. And the problem is: I know what happens now. I know exactly how much pain I'll be in…and I'm afraid, and the fear's bigger than the pain, bigger than the blimp sailing through the night sky above us, like a portal to another world.

SERGEI: I love my Galina, but sometimes you need to put your foot on the pedal. You need to put your dick where it doesn't belong. This is the nature of want. It takes you crazy places. And it revs you up, like motorboat. I take my game, and Tim Porter is left in my wake. 3-2.

Scoreboard: Set # 4; S. Sergeyev 3-2.

TIM: I am overwhelmed. The next one is the worst. We're at the doctor's. Mallory is eight months pregnant. Eight. She's been on bed-rest for a month, a month when Angie couldn't spare her, so she let her go, and, well, let's just say that didn't go over well. She's lying on the table—just a routine thing. The doctor's putting that goop all over her belly. She's lubing Mal right up, like an old engine.

MALLORY: *(Not worried, just chatting.)* I haven't felt her moving all that much today, you know.

TIM: The doctor smiled and nodded. Nothing to be worried about.

MALLORY: She's usually such a kicker. She jabs me everywhere. I can't fall asleep she jabs me so much.

TIM: The doctor's smiling and nodding, smiling and nodding. Then she leaves the room, just abruptly. Just like that.

MALLORY: Where'd she go?

TIM: I don't know.

MALLORY: Tim, where'd she go? Why'd she leave like that?

TIM: I don't know.

MALLORY: I don't like that.

TIM: It's fine.

MALLORY: What if it's not fine?

TIM: Don't assume that.

MALLORY: Where'd she go, Tim? Why isn't she coming back??

SERGEI: So I put my foot on the gas! All the wanting, all the loss, all the work, coming together like car screeching around a curve. It must take shortest fastest route possible to get where it is going but as a result it might crash along the way. It might burn whatever is in its path. I am up 4-2 now, and Tim Porter is what is in my path.

TIM: And then she did come back. And she came back with another, older doctor. And they both listened again for the baby's heartbeat.
And it wasn't there.

MALLORY: What do you mean it's not there? That can't be. I mean, it's there. Maybe she's just sleeping and it's really quiet. Can that happen? Can she just go to sleep?

TIM: Of course they did tests, and of course they waited to tell us, but they knew. I think they knew right away that she was gone.

MALLORY: That's not possible. I walked four miles every day. I drank foul green juice. I made sure I gained enough weight but not too much. I did yoga, kegels. I slept well. I did everything right.

TIM: I didn't know you did all that.

MALLORY: It's my fault. It knew – somehow it knew I wasn't good enough. That I wasn't sure I really wanted it.

TIM: That's not true.

MALLORY: I'm dying, Tim. I'm dying. This is…I can't do it… it's too much.

TIM: They told her she'd have to have the baby. You know, like have it anyway. Go through labor. Better for the body. Safer.

MALLORY: *(Pleading with him and then breaking down.)* You have it. I can't have it. You have it. I can't. I can't. I can't.

SERGEI: I can't stop. I move Tim Porter around court like puppet. He is in pain. But one must take advantage. And I do. I go up 5-2 in fourth set.

TIM: It is silent. It's just…silent when your wife delivers a baby that isn't going to…You hear every sound in a room that feels enormous but still isn't big enough to hold your…I mean, it's just…silent.

SERGEI: Sometimes the ball is cleanly and clearly in and sometimes it just clips tiny fraction of the line. But either way it is in. It is this kind of ball that gets me the set.

GALINA: Incredible, Sergei.

SERGEI: Did you hear that? I win! Fourth set. Where are you, Tim Porter?

> *Scoreboard: Set # 4; S. Sergeyev 6-2*
>
> *Set # 5, 0-0*
>
> *Both men take a break, too unsettled for different reasons even to sit.*

SERGEI: We start the fifth set! And I can tell Tim is in pain.

TIM: All tied up, two sets apiece. But really we're not even.

SERGEI: He is leaning on his racquet between points as though it could support him.

TIM: I feel like I'm going to die on this court.

SERGEI: First to six. That's what we're down to.

TIM: The cortisone is gone. The adrenaline is gone. And the pressure in my back is building, growing, expanding, tighter and tighter.

GALINA: A handful of games. And your life will change.

SERGEI: I am serving in the first game of the set at 40-30 and I hit an ace. An awesome ace. A whoosh.

TIM: I don't even see it; it's that fast.

SERGEI: He is bent over when I serve; he wouldn't have gotten to the ball if I'd hit it right to him. But still – he raises his hand.

TIM: Review.

SERGEI: Excuse me?

TIM: I'd like a review.

SERGEI: A desperation move. But it doesn't matter. They review it and according to their cameras–

TIM: It's out.

SERGEI: What??? One millimeter from the line. And I am: "You've gotta to be kidding me." I'm shouting: "really? Really??!" I am outraged. I don't know where it comes from.

TIM: I assume you're trying to pump yourself up.

SERGEI: I am not trying to do anything. I am out of control. I don't understand how something that felt that good could have been out.

TIM: I look at Drobek. He looks at me. He shrugs. It's like Sergei's *asking* for the point to be taken away. And so he takes it away. Deuce.

SERGEI: But I am sick of things being taken away. Everything in my life is slippery through my fingers. Isn't there anything I can just keep?

GALINA: What do you mean you want to go to a diner?

SERGEI: This is yesterday.

GALINA: I think diners are not very nice. I do not like to use the restroom at such places.

SERGEI: Come on, Lina.

GALINA: And you will ruin your dinner. We are going for such a nice dinner. Don't ruin it.

SERGEI: I will not ruin my dinner. I promise.

GALINA: I will want to get French fries at a diner and then I won't fit into my new dress to wear to dinner tonight.

SERGEI: I would love for you to eat a million French fries but I don't think you will ever eat even one.

GALINA: Why do you want to go so badly to this diner?

SERGEI: I need a grilled cheese sandwich with bacon and a cup of watery chicken soup with those little crackers you crumble inside it. Whenever I am in New York City for United States Open, I have this meal.

GALINA: Well, you have yet to win United States Open so maybe is not such good luck.

SERGEI: Please.

GALINA: Fine, okay. But you will note that it is under duress that I go.

SERGEI: When we get to the diner, I order some French fries. They sit on table untouched.

GALINA: Okay, you have had your grilled cheese with bacon and your watery soup and maybe we can go now? We should rest before dinner. You need to conserve your energy.

SERGEI: What do you think might happen at dinner tonight, Lina?

GALINA: What do you mean by that?

SERGEI: Are you expecting any kind of special event?

GALINA: I am expecting to get annoyed by you a number of times, which would make it not special at all, but quite ordinary.

SERGEI: You don't think I might be taking you out to such a fancy dinner for a purpose?

GALINA: What purpose?

SERGEI: Galina didn't know it, but I had been looking at rings. I had very secretly spoken with diamond dealer. I'd been researching. Cut. Clarity. Grade. At first I said, I want A++ diamond! And they said, no, that is not actually how it works.

GALINA: You're full of shit, Sergei, you know that?

SERGEI: I know you love me, my honey bunny.

GALINA: What of it.

SERGEI: And I love you. Against all my better judgment.

GALINA: Wow, you really know how to flatter a girl.

SERGEI: And so I want you to eat this French fry.

> *He holds one out to her.*

GALINA: But I am not hungry.

SERGEI: I don't care whether or not you are hungry. I want you to eat it because I want to see that the woman I will marry is capable of enjoying this world. Of taking what it has to give.

GALINA: Oh, you will marry me. Is that right?

SERGEI: That's right. And this is no test since I know you will pass it. But the thing is, Galina, my love, this life has a lot of miseries on offer. It is like this diner's menu—

> *He holds it up.*

It is enormous and it is thick with miseries. But occasionally there is daily special. And it is not only made fresh that day, it is good price too! And you have to get it when you see it. You have to buy it and you have to eat it, immediately.

GALINA: This French fry is now standing in for some idea so big I am not sure I understand it.

SERGEI: You are already perfect. Stop working so hard. Relax, for once! What are you hoping to be? You are what I want. And what I will always want, even if you say this is impossible. I believe it is possible. I believe I believe I believe.

GALINA: Hilarious. Sergei.

SERGEI: No, I'm serious.

> *He gets down on one knee and holds out a ring.*

I am asking you, Galina, to marry me.

> *Beat.*

GALINA: Here?!

SERGEI: Here. At this very diner. Isn't it funny and surprising?

GALINA: Do I look like I am laughing??

SERGEI: No, you do not appear to be laughing.

> *In fact, she is crying. She looks at SERGEI, holding out the ring.*

> *But instead—she eats a French fry. Slowly. SERGEI stands and holds her.*

GALINA: I will marry you on the condition that we never go to a diner again.

SERGEI: But we will always go to diners. Now they will be special reminders of our beautiful engagement story.

GALINA: Fuck you, Sergei.

SERGEI: Thank you, my love.

> *He slides the ring on her finger.*

And then we were engaged, and we went to shi-shi restaurant—very fancy—to celebrate, and I was so happy: I am going to be MARRIED!... Until I came home to sleep, at which point, I could not stop thinking: my parents will never know my wife. And worse: my wife—my children—will never know my parents. It is as though they never existed. They are not here watching most important match of my life, which I am throwing out the window like baby with so much bathwater.

GALINA: Sergei, you must recover from stupid docked point. It is nothing. Move on.

SERGEI: But I am not so good at recovery. Perhaps, when I am docked point, things like this, small small things, it is like reopening wound that has not had chance to heal. And so is painful. And I lose myself in this pain.

> *Scoreboard: Set # 5; T. Porter 2-0.*

TIM: I break his serve and then take the second game real quick. I am in so much pain I can't think; I just get inside a rhythm and stay there.

Beat.

Rhythm. That's what it is. When you lose a baby the way we did, and then even though you can't bear it, you make love to try to make another baby, it's rhythm.

SERGEI: There is something addictive about this pain. There is some way in which you cannot let it go. You hoard it. You keep it like most prized possession.

TIM: But it doesn't work. Eventually we try In Vitro.

MALLORY: I hate you, Tim.

TIM: This is what it's like every day.

MALLORY: *(More tired than she's ever been.)* I hate you, Tim, and I regret the day I met you.

TIM: Thanks, honey.

MALLORY: My ass is so sore you don't understand.

TIM: I'm sorry.

MALLORY: You should be.

TIM: Mallory.

MALLORY: Yeah.

TIM: I think you're very brave.

SERGEI: It would be very brave to let go of this pain. To live without it holding your hand. It would mean being responsible for all that you do and all that you are. It would mean being alone.

MALLORY: Fuck you, Tim. I don't wanna be brave. This sucks. Just say that this sucks.

TIM: It sucks.

MALLORY: Mean it.

TIM: It sucks!! What do you want me to say? You think I've been having such a great time? No…The pressure to… All the pressure it builds up and all of a sudden my whole body, my back, is…

MALLORY: So it's my fault you have a bad back?

TIM: It's no one's fault. It just is! The pressure is too much. To be "Tim Porter." To stay good at a game that requires so much focus, all the time, and these guys coming up with better bodies, faster–

MALLORY: It's always about the tennis. Isn't it.

TIM: Yes, tennis is a big part of my life. I think you knew that comin' in.

MALLORY: I don't know what I knew. Maybe I just liked you because you were famous and you seemed to like me.

TIM: You can be a real bitch when you wanna be, you know that?

MALLORY: That must put a lot of pressure on you. To have to deal with such a bitch all the time. Or maybe that's why you're barely here.

TIM: I'm barely here because I'm out there working my ass off for *us*.

MALLORY: No, you're running away from us, because you can, but I can't: I'm home alone with nothing to do because I lost my job because I was pregnant with a baby that *died* so you'll forgive me if I'm a little touchy every now and then.

TIM: Look, I know how hard this has been for you–

MALLORY: You don't know! You have no idea. None. Zero.

TIM: Oh I have no idea? I have no idea? I haven't experienced any loss?? Any fucking heartbreaking loss? Is that right, Mallory?

MALLORY: That's right!

TIM: *(Shouting now.)* Well then fuck you!! Just…fuck you.

> *(His back goes out.)*

Oh shit.

> *(In silence, MALLORY rubs his back a bit. TIM cries out in pain a couple times. Maybe he cries, quietly.)*

TIM: *(Quietly, he's broken up.)* It makes me wanna die what's happened. It makes me not believe in God. It makes me not have faith in all the things I used to have faith in.

MALLORY: Like what.

TIM: I don't know.

>*Then, very simply.*

That life would turn out okay.

MALLORY: You have a pretty storybook life, Timmy, according to most of the world.

TIM: It would be a big deal never to be a dad.

MALLORY: Then leave me. Leave me and find someone who can give you a kid.

>*He turns around, even though it pains him.*

TIM: I would never do that.

MALLORY: I'm scared for it to work, Tim…I'm not ready. I still feel like someone owes *me* a great childhood. I'm still waiting, you know?

TIM: I'm so sorry you feel that way. I wish you didn't.

MALLORY: I don't know anymore why people wanna be parents. I think there's something wrong with me.

TIM: Honey…I've done as well in the life I chose as anyone can hope for. But I still think, or *hope*, hope to god, that maybe there are moments of being a parent when you're like: this is it. *This* is what it's about: watching your own kid grow up.

MALLORY: Then be with me. Really be with me. We'll find out together.

TIM: We will. I just need one more slam.

MALLORY: *(Really asking him.)* Why, though?

TIM: Because I know that I can win one more.

MALLORY: I knew that I would have a baby. I knew I would be number one in the world…I knew I would never look back when I stopped playing. But knowing those things didn't make them happen.

TIM: *(To the audience.)* I once went on a date with this woman who asked me if I had to choose one, I'd pick fame or money. City or countryside, sex or food…those kinds of questions. Then she asked whether I'd pick tennis or my family, and I swear to God I stood up and left. I mean, what kind of question is that? I kept thinking no one would ever be asked to make that choice.

SERGEI: And this is what makes you the gigantic asshole that you are, Tim Porter. Because you do not even *realize* the choice you have made.

MALLORY: *(To the audience, conflicted.)* The in vitro works.

It works.

SERGEI: I made same choice, just a child, not knowing the finality of this choice that I was making.

MALLORY: When the doctor tells us…

TIM: Oh, honey. It's wonderful. Please see that.

GALINA: After we get engaged, I say Sergei, let's call my mother. He says, but you do not even like your mother, why should we call her right away with our private happy news? And I think about that. It is not often that Sergei should stump me with a question.

MALLORY: I wake up every morning expecting it to end.

GALINA: And then he says: you know, you are lucky. At least you know your mother well enough to dislike her.

MALLORY: It keeps going. I hurt everywhere and I can't even lie down. I weep at commercials on TV. I weep when I see mothers struggling with their children. I'm enormous; I catch sight of my shadow and I don't know myself. It's spring and I'm huge; I've just been consuming time.

SERGEI: I serve at love two, and I want. I want and I want and I want and I want. There are thousands of people here tonight and if each one represented one of my wants, there would still not be enough.

TIM: How do you get to the bottom of wanting? Is there *any* end to what we want? What we can't have? What we're searching for?

SERGEI: I want to justify all the sacrifices. I want to be faithful to my wife. I want to have sex with all the women of the world. I want to die. I want to live. I want to say goodbye to my parents. I never want to say goodbye.

MALLORY: When I am near the end of my labor, I lose the instinct to push. Something is holding me back and at first I don't know what it is – and then I do.

SERGEI: So what can I do? I picture their faces while I still can and I take each ball, one at a time. This one is a way of saying I miss you. This one is a way of saying I love you. This one is a way of saying why did you never teach me to cook even the simplest thing? This one is a way of saying I am aware of the bad breath I have inherited from my father and I freshen my mouth whenever I can.

MALLORY: I know all of a sudden that I will die. And I know with equal certainty that I am bringing a person into the world who will also die. And this feels…

SERGEI: This ball is the fish with bitter lemon my mother used to make for dinner. I didn't like it. It's good for you, she always said. It's good for you, Sergei. Eat. Eat as much as you can. Get so full with life you could die.

MALLORY: And then with one enormous whoosh I decide to push anyway, to meet my son, because what else can you do; you are only alive this once.

SERGEI: This one is a way of saying fuck you for leaving me. Fuck you for teaching me with your last lesson that we are all alone.

GALINA: No, it's enough, Sergei. It's enough. You let this go now.

SERGEI: I can't.

GALINA: But you are not alone! Don't you remember? I said yes. I said "I love you too." I said "you are right, we don't need to call my mother right now. You are all I need." I said "don't you know there is occasionally daily special? And it is not only made fresh that day, it is good price! And so you have to get it when you see it. You have to buy it and you have to eat it, immediately."

SERGEI: *I* said that!

GALINA: Then do it!!

This is your chance, Sergei. Do it. Now. You are right here; it's right in front of you.

MALLORY: *(With wonder.)* He's here.

TIM: He's here!

SERGEI: I'm here.

GALINA: Yes.

MALLORY: He's here. He sloshed out of me like a gigantic fish. And all the pain – everything that came before – recedes. Until all that's left is joy.

TIM: But I wasn't there.

MALLORY: It's not possible he's here. And it's also not possible he was ever *not* here.

TIM: I was in the middle of a first round match at Wimbledon against a not very good eighteen-year-old from Galveston Texas. I didn't stop when I saw Mallory leave my box, two days from her due date. I kept playing.

MALLORY: *(Not accusatory, just a statement of fact.)* You weren't there.

GALINA: You are here, Sergei. And you are alive.

TIM: And I lost. I lost the match anyway.

SERGEI: *(A realization.)* I am alive.

TIM: You asshole, Tim. You loser. You asshole.

SERGEI: *(A huge release.)* I glance at my Galina and her eyes are sparkling. Did I mention that no one has eyes such as hers? I go up 4-2 and suddenly it is just a joy to be playing. To be hitting a ball at such speeds and with such precision. This *is* my strength, after all.

TIM: *(To MALLORY.)* I'm sorry, Mallory. I'm *so* sorry. But I have to play.

If I stop, I don't know who I am.

MALLORY: *(Firmly but with affection.)* Come on, Tim Porter. You're Mallory Sinclair's husband; that's who you are.

TIM: *(Laughing.)* Well, that's true. I am that…I am that.

SERGEI: Tim is crouching behind the baseline, laughing or crying – I can't tell which. I am moving him around court like dog on leash and somehow he finds this hilarious.

MALLORY: You can do it, Timmy. And we will love you even when you're old. When no one talks about you on TV anymore. When they can't even remember your name.

TIM: *(A realization.)* I am as young now as I'll ever be for the rest of my life. So why not just play.

SERGEI: He serves a very good game. Close points. We're running everywhere.

TIM: Wild, looping, batshit crazy shots. And some of them go in. Enough of them.

SERGEI: He pulls even with me in the set.

TIM: Four all.

SERGEI/MALLORY/GALINA: Four all.

GALINA: The match is so close, and yet – I feel relaxed. Like bird flying light on the wind, maybe. Like I have, for moment, escaped my own death. It is the way I will feel when we have children, children who want for nothing and yet are still unhappy, because at this point it will occur to me that everyone is just unhappy. And for some reason this frees me. And I start to truly enjoy myself.

TIM: I gave him my name. So one day he'll be a man named Tim Porter, just like his dad and his dad's dad. But now, he's two months old and we stand at the window; we can see the Statue of Liberty down the river, bathed in the colors of the setting sun.

MALLORY: Why is it that as soon as a baby is born he doesn't wanna go to sleep? What is it that we know before we know it?

SERGEI: There is, at the bottom of everything, an emptiness. We do what we can to run from this. Tree after tree after tree.

TIM: And then Sergei hits the most beautiful backhand of the match and when I look across the net I see that he's crying. I've never seen anything like it. He's sobbing. And hitting balls past me, left and then right.

GALINA: He's crying. My Sergei. And the way he is playing, I know for certain that he will fulfill his destiny. He plays like he belongs on this court, like it is his, *finally*…Like he deserves it.

SERGEI: For first time *ever*, it is like we are dancing *together* – me and Tim Porter.

TIM: Just rhythm. Just a pulse of rhythm.

SERGEI: You go back to basics. / Feet apart, racquet back, contact.

TIM: Feet apart, racquet back, contact. Just like you did when you were ten-years-old.

SERGEI: I go up 5-4. And you start to feel it. Just a little. Just a glimmer. The light at the end of the tunnel.

TIM: *(Contemplative.)* It is fast and slow all at once.

SERGEI: He serves, and it is the mark of champion that in this circumstance, where the pressure is immense, he holds for 5-all.

TIM: See, sometimes it's just about tennis. Just about the body.

SERGEI: I throw the ball up; I see it against the lights, against the night sky; I slam it down. I don't have to look; I know it skids off the line and into the darkness. Unhittable.

TIM: 15-love. Sergei.

SERGEI: 30-love. Then 30-15.

TIM: What would I take with me if I could? The sounds of the crowd, for sure. That one guy who yells "Porter!" *after* the ref calls for quiet.

The first minute after winning a huge match when the rush is…well, indescribable.

(Beat, then sadly.)

My childhood. I'd keep that if I could…
I mean, heck…it's a shame we get old.

SERGEI: At 30-15, I taste it. It is sour and it is sweet and I want it so badly, it hurts.

TIM: I whip one past you. 30-all.

SERGEI: But then I pass you down the line. 40-30.

TIM: I leaked the rumor. Of my own retirement. I think I wanted to see how it would feel. To try it on. Like a hat you know you'll wear one day.

SERGEI: Then it is deuce. / Fucking deuce—

TIM: Fucking deuce—

SERGEI: At 5-all in the fifth set. I can't believe it. And yet somehow it is always deuce. One is always tied up, tied together, with the other person, no one ahead or behind.

TIM: Do you know how many matches I've played? This is all I've done. This is what I've done with my life.

SERGEI: Deuce. Always deuce. Another deuce.

TIM: *(A quick stream-of-consciousness.)* "Tim" someone calls out. "Tim!" As if they know me. And then we are in the middle of the point and my feet are moving and my mind is on overdrive and there are a ton of stars above our heads and it's the middle of the night and it's the middle of my life only it's the end, and my son is already grown, and my parents have been gone many years and I am old; I am no longer a boy.

(A sad realization, and now we slow down.)

I am no longer a boy…

I've loved this game, every second. But now I hold Timmy in my arms by the window, a different Timmy than he was even yesterday—this is how quickly he changes; every day he is a *new boy*—and the autumn sun's setting and the sky's full of all these crazy colors and they spread out on the river, like a wreath, like a halo of light. Like the end and the beginning of everything.

> *(TIM and SERGEI play on, the sounds of the cheering crowd and of the ball being hit reverberating faster and faster as the lights fade.)*

PHOTOGRAPH 51

Characters

ROSALIND FRANKLIN
a scientist in her 30s; she's brilliant, always on her
toes, and doesn't suffer fools

MAURICE WILKINS
a scientist in his 30s or 40s; he's formal and polite,
refined, restrained, gentle and wounded

RAY GOSLING
a scientist in his 20s; he's awkward, endearing,
sweet, lacking in confidence

DON CASPAR
a scientist in his 20s or 30s; he's open, affable,
humble and honest

JAMES WATSON
a scientist in his early 20s; he's all confidence,
arrogance, hunger and drive

FRANCIS CRICK
a scientist in his 30s or 40s; he's very proper,
not unkind, brash, a comedian philosopher, who
enjoys being the center of attention

Setting
Many and various. The simpler the set, the more
fluidly the action can move forward.

Note
This play is based on the story of the race to the
double helix in England in the years between
1951 and 1953, but is a work of fiction. I have
altered timelines, facts and events, and recreated
characters for dramatic purposes.

Photograph 51 had its New York premiere at the Ensemble Studio Theatre (William Carden, Artistic Director), a production sponsored and developed by the Ensemble Studio Theatre/ Alfred P. Sloan Foundation Science & Technology Project where it opened on November 1, 2010. The director was Linsay Firman, the stage manager Danielle Buccino, the set designer Nick Francone, the costume designer Suzanne Chesney, the lighting designer Les Dickert, and the sound designer Shane Rettig. The cast was as follows:

ROSALIND FRANKLIN	Kristen Bush
MAURICE WILKINS	Kevin Collins
RAY GOSLING	David Gelles
DON CASPAR	Benjamin Pelteson
JAMES WATSON	Haskell King
FRANCIS CRICK	Jeremy Webb

Photograph 51 was subsequently produced by the Michael Grandage Company at the Noël Coward Theatre, West End, London, opening on September 14, 2015. The director was Michael Grandage, the stage manager Howard Jepson, the set and costume designer Christopher Oram, the lighting designer Neil Austin, and the sound designer Adam Cork. The cast was as follows:

ROSALIND FRANKLIN	Nicole Kidman
MAURICE WILKINS	Stephen Campbell Moore
RAY GOSLING	Joshua Silver
DON CASPAR	Patrick Kennedy
JAMES WATSON	Will Attenborough
FRANCIS CRICK	Edward Bennett

Photograph 51 was originally commissioned and produced by Active Cultures, the vernacular theatre of Maryland (Mary Resing, Director), opening on February 10, 2008.

This play is the winner of the 2008 STAGE International Script Competition and was developed, in part, through the University of California, Santa Barbara's STAGE Project by the Professional Artists Lab (Nancy Kawalek, Director) and the California NanoSystems Institute.

Certain things exist outside of time. It was ten years ago, it was this morning…It happened in the past and it was always happening. It happened every single minute of the day…

*

He felt like he was seeing greatness, like he was in the room watching Watson and Crick put the final touches on their model of DNA, or maybe he was seeing Rosalind Franklin with her magnificent X-rays. Wasn't it the girl, after all, who had actually found the key to life?

Ann Patchett, *Run*

As scientists understand very well, personality has always been an inseparable part of their styles of inquiry and a potent, if unacknowledged, factor in their results. Indeed, no art or popular entertainment is so carefully built as is science upon the individual talents, preferences and habits of its leaders.

Horace Judson, *The Eighth Day of Creation*

The lights rise on ROSALIND.

ROSALIND: This is what it was like. We made the invisible visible. We could see atoms, not only see them—manipulate them, move them around. We were so powerful. Our instruments felt like extensions of our own bodies. We could see everything, really see it – except, sometimes, what was right in front of us.

When I was a child I used to draw shapes. Shapes overlapping, like endless Venn diagrams. My parents said, "Rosalind, maybe you should draw people? Don't you want to draw our family? Our little dog?" I didn't. I drew patterns of the tiniest repeating structures. In my mind were patterns of the tiniest repeating structures.

WILKINS: It was a particularly cold winter in London. January 1951.

ROSALIND: And when I first got to use my father's camera, I went outside and found four leaves. I arranged them carefully, on the curb. But the photograph I took was not of leaves. You see, nothing is ever just one thing. This was the world, a map of rivers and mountain ranges in endless repetition. And when I told my father I wanted to become a scientist, he said, "Ah. I see."…Then he said "No."

WILKINS: And at the same time, in Paris–

WATSON: Not again, Wilkins. Really?

WILKINS: In Paris, Rosalind Franklin was saying her goodbyes.

WATSON: I promise it'll end the same way.

WILKINS: *(Ignoring him.)* There was a party for her at the Laboratoire Centrale. Everyone stayed late into the night, drinking and telling stories, entreating her not to leave.

CRICK: *(To the audience.)* But she'd just won a fellowship at King's College London and one didn't turn down a job at King's—especially since there was a chance she'd get to work in the field of genetics–

CASPAR: A field in which the possibilities were…well, they were endless. In which the promise of personal and professional fulfillment was tangible.

WILKINS: *(To CASPAR, sharply.)* What are you doing here?

GOSLING: So she wrote a…polite letter requesting the instruments she'd require:

ROSALIND: *(Writing the letter, cold and formal.)* I require an X-ray generating tube. And a camera specially made so that the temperature inside it can be carefully controlled. Otherwise, the solution will change during its exposure, and Dr. Wilkins you know as well as I do that that just won't do. Finally, if at all possible, I'd like to know when this order will be placed so that, if need be, I can request a few minor modifications. Yours sincerely, Dr. Rosalind Franklin.

WILKINS: Dear Miss Franklin, you are ever so…cordial. But I must warn you—we at King's are very serious. So serious, in fact, and intent on being at "the cutting edge" as they say, that we will be moving your research into another area entirely.

WILKINS and ROSALIND at King's together.

ROSALIND: I beg your pardon?

WILKINS: Yes, instead of proteins you will be working on deciphering the structure of DNA.

ROSALIND: Is that so.

WILKINS: You see, I recently took X-ray photos of DNA that came out remarkably well, showing that it is unmistakably crystalline in shape. Therefore it now seems evident that King's needs to push forward in determining, through crystallography, at which you are quite expert—

ROSALIND: Thank you. I am.

WILKINS: *(Thrown for a moment.)* …Yes. No one will argue with that. *(Beat.)* At any rate, we need to push forward in determining why it is that in the chromosome the numbers of purines and pyrimidines come in pairs. So that we can then determine how replication works. So that we can then determine—

ROSALIND: I know what you're talking about.

WILKINS: Yes, yes I suppose you do. Then I'll leap straight to the point. You will be assisting me in my study of the

Signer DNA from Switzerland. Everyone wanted it and yet somehow Randall got it. The old rogue. I don't know how he did it…

ROSALIND: *(Icy.)* I don't think I heard you right.

WILKINS: You did! We have the Signer stock. Quite a coup really. When you think about it.

ROSALIND: But did you say *I'd* be assisting *you*?

WILKINS: Yes! …And my doctoral student, Ray Gosling, will assist *you.*

GOSLING: *(Putting out his hand, which ROSALIND ignores.)* Hello!

ROSALIND: But…Randall told me I'd be heading up the study. That I'd be in charge of my own work here. Surely, there's been some misunderstanding.

WILKINS: No. No misunderstanding. Circumstances changed. You see…we now feel that if we discover *this* structure—this structure—we could discover the way the world works, Miss Franklin. What some are calling "the secret of life." Can you imagine that?

ROSALIND: Dr. Wilkins, I will not be anyone's assistant.

> *Beat.*

WILKINS: What was that?

ROSALIND: I don't like others to analyze *my* data, *my* work. I work best when I work alone. If, for whatever reason, I am forced into a different situation, I should feel that I came here under false pretenses.

WILKINS: I see… *(Giving this some thought.)* Then perhaps we could think of our work together as a kind of partnership. Surely that will suit you?

ROSALIND: I don't suppose it matters whether or not it suits me, does it?

> *She exits.*

GOSLING: Well, that went well.

WATSON: See? She was meant to be Wilkins' *assistant,* and therein lay the problem. She misunderstood the terms.

And after that, the rest was inevitable. The race lost right there. In a single moment.

WILKINS: No—nothing is inevitable.

CASPAR: She would never have left Paris to be someone's subordinate. She was quite clear with me about that.

CRICK: Well, that's not what we heard.

CASPAR: You heard what you wanted to hear. One of those specialties of human nature.

WILKINS: Is it really absolutely necessary that you be here too?

GOSLING: Anyway! We began. It was gray in London in January. We were working in a...well, it must be said, dank cellar in the Strand. There were no two ways about that.

> *ROSALIND, WILKINS and GOSLING are spread out in the lab, working.*

ROSALIND: Could it be any gloomier here? As your *partner*, I might entreat you to find us a more hospitable working environment.

WILKINS: Labs are more nicely appointed in Paris, then?

ROSALIND: There's no comparison.

WILKINS: You know, not all of us felt we should leave England when she needed us most.

ROSALIND: Thank you, Dr. Wilkins, for your patriotic spirit. I can assure you, however, that I was doing much more for British society after the war by working on coal molecules in France than I would have had I been in London eating rationed food and parking my car on a site cleared by a bomb that used to be someone's home.

WILKINS: I was only joking—really.

GOSLING: *(Trying to lighten the situation.)* It's true—he's quite the jokester.

ROSALIND: And aren't you the same Wilkins who worked on the Manhattan Project in *California* during the war?

WILKINS: *(Proudly.)* For a few months' time, yes.

ROSALIND: Maybe you're aware of the fact that not a single female scientist from Britain was given a research position during wartime?

WILKINS: Is that so.

ROSALIND: I'll have you know that nuclear force is not something of which I approve.

WILKINS: Then I suppose it's good no one asked you to work on it.

ROSALIND: I beg your pardon?

WILKINS: *(Attempting to joke.)* At any rate, you lot never do seem to approve of it.

ROSALIND: I'm not sure I understand what you're driving at.

GOSLING: No, he—

WILKINS: All I meant was—the irony of...

ROSALIND: What irony?

WILKINS: *(Without apology.)* Just that...people...worked hard to...come up with these ways to save...well, the Jews, and then all you hear back from them is how they don't approve. It feels a little...

ROSALIND: You're absolutely right that the Jews should be in a more grateful frame of mind these days.

WILKINS: All right, Rosy.

ROSALIND: My name is Rosalind. But you can call me Miss Franklin. Everyone else does.

WILKINS: Fine.

ROSALIND: Of course I'd prefer Dr. Franklin but that doesn't seem to be done here, does it, Mr. Wilkins?

WILKINS: Dr. Wilkins.

ROSALIND: Dr. Wilkins, I don't joke. I take my work seriously as I trust you do too.

WILKINS: Of course I do.

> *Long beat.*

GOSLING: How do you like that—it's nearly two already.

WILKINS: No need for constant updates on the time, Gosling. There's a clock right there that we can see perfectly well—

GOSLING: No…I was just saying, or, I mean, suggesting, that perhaps we might take our lunch?

ROSALIND: We've been having so much fun that the time has really flown, hasn't it, Dr. Wilkins?

WILKINS: Has it.

ROSALIND: So where shall we go? I'm famished, actually.

>*WILKINS starts to leave; he's off to lunch.*

Dr. Wilkins?

WILKINS: *(Turning back.)* Hm?

>*Off her look.*

Oh, I'd love to have lunch, but…

ROSALIND: But what?

WILKINS: *(Matter-of-fact.)* I eat in the senior common room.

ROSALIND: That's where we'll go then.

WILKINS: That's the thing.

ROSALIND: What's the *thing*?

WILKINS: It's for men only.

ROSALIND: Is that so.

WILKINS: It is.

>*Beat.*

ROSALIND: Well go to it then.

WILKINS: If you're sure.

ROSALIND: Absolutely.

WILKINS: All right then.

GOSLING: *(To the audience.)* The next hour was…well, it wasn't what you'd traditionally think of as fun.

ROSALIND: It's absurd, isn't it? Archaic!

GOSLING: What is?

ROSALIND: Well, this business of the senior common room, of course.

GOSLING: I suppose. But…you can't worry about it.

ROSALIND: I can worry over whatever I choose to worry over, Mr. Gosling!

GOSLING: It's not like biophysicists have such great conversations at meals anyway. They tend just to talk about the work. They never take a break.

ROSALIND: But those are precisely the conversations I need to have. Scientists make discoveries over lunch.

GOSLING: If you say so.

ROSALIND: Can I ask you a question?

GOSLING: Of course.

ROSALIND: What's he like—Wilkins. You've worked for him for a few years, haven't you?

GOSLING: And now they've moved me along to you. The conveyer belt chugs along. But doctoral students are good people to work with. We're like liquids—we take the shape of the vessel into which we're poured.

ROSALIND: What do you mean by that?

GOSLING: That you don't have to worry about a thing: my allegiance will be to you. You're my advisor now.

ROSALIND: *(Taken aback.)* Well, good. I would have expected as much.

GOSLING: Wilkins is fine. Between you and me he's a bit of a stiff, but I'm sure you two will get along. He's easy enough to get along with. And he works hard. You know, no wife to go home to, no children. He devotes himself completely.

ROSALIND: So do I.

GOSLING: What does Mr. Franklin have to say about that?

ROSALIND: *(Archly.)* There is no Mr. Franklin. Unless, of course, you're referring to my father.

Beat.

GOSLING: No. I wasn't. I'm sorry. I really didn't mean to offend. I didn't mean to–

WILKINS entering, cutting GOSLING off.

ROSALIND: And how was your lunch, Dr. Wilkins?

WILKINS: Just fine. Thank you for asking.

ROSALIND: I'm glad that on my first day here you didn't take a break from your daily routine to accompany me somewhere I was permitted to dine.

WILKINS: Miss Franklin…Let me be clear about something: I was looking forward to your arrival here.

GOSLING: He truly was.

WILKINS: That's enough, Gosling.

GOSLING: But you talked about it all the time–how her chemistry and your theory would be a perfect marriage of–

ROSALIND: My chemistry and your theory? Are you suggesting I don't have theory, Dr. Wilkins?

WILKINS: Of course not.

ROSALIND: Good.

GOSLING: He was just fantasizing about a life free of all the menial tasks associated with biochemistry–

WILKINS: Gosling!

ROSALIND: Menial?

WILKINS: No! And all I wanted to say was that I don't like that things have got off to a…rocky start. I'd like to begin again.

Beat.

ROSALIND: All right.

WILKINS: All right?

WILKINS puts out his hand to shake, and she does grudgingly.

ROSALIND: I'm Dr. Rosalind Franklin. It's a pleasure to meet you.

WILKINS: It's a pleasure to meet you too.

ROSALIND: I've heard so much about you.

WILKINS: And I you.

GOSLING: Hi–I'm Ray Gosling. I'll be your doctoral student.

WILKINS: Unnecessary, Gosling.

ROSALIND: Yes, Gosling, *we've* already met.

WILKINS: May I ask you, Miss Franklin, what you're most looking forward to here at King's?

ROSALIND: I think, Dr. Wilkins, I'm looking forward to dispensing with these games at which point I can begin taking photographs of crystals of DNA. It wasn't what I came here to do but if we want to discover the secret of life as you put it, I'll do it with the cameras I choose from what's here and the sample from the Signer stock. You can use whatever's left and come reintroduce yourself to me whenever you'd like.

    ROSALIND exits.

WILKINS: I see.

CASPAR: Did it really happen that way? Were you quite so...

WILKINS: I wasn't anything. I was perfectly fine...

    To GOSLING.

A bit of a stiff perhaps, but otherwise...

GOSLING: Oh did you hear that bit?

WILKINS: *(Annoyed.)* Yes, I heard "that bit."

CRICK: Well, *I* don't think you're at all...You're not at all... well, all right you can be quite stiff, if you don't mind my saying.

WILKINS: *(Sarcastic.)* Why ever would I mind?

    ROSALIND entering

ROSALIND: Good morning, Dr. Wilkins.

WILKINS: Good morning, Miss Franklin.

ROSALIND: Did you have a nice weekend?

WILKINS: It was fine, I suppose.

    Beat.

How was yours?

ROSALIND: Fine.

WILKINS: Did you do anything interesting?

ROSALIND: Yesterday I went to the matinee of *The Winter's Tale* at the Phoenix. Peter Brook directed it.

WILKINS: That's funny.

ROSALIND: Why is that funny?

WILKINS: I almost went to see the very same performance. I was in the vicinity, walking, and I passed the Phoenix and I very nearly went in.

ROSALIND: It was sold out?

WILKINS: No. I never got that far.

ROSALIND: Then where's the coincidence?

WILKINS: It's just that…our paths so nearly crossed.

    Beat.

Was it any good?

ROSALIND: Oh yes. Very.

WILKINS: The great difference, you know, between *The Winter's Tale* and the story on which it's based—Pandosto—is that in Shakespeare's version the heroine survives.

ROSALIND: John Gielgud played Leontes. He really was very good. Very lifelike. Very good. When Hermione died, even though it was his fault, I felt for him. I truly did.

WILKINS: And who played Hermione?

ROSALIND: I don't remember. She didn't stand out, I suppose.

WILKINS: My favorite part, you know, is Antigonus's dream.

ROSALIND: Why?

WILKINS: Because even though Hermione tells him to name her child Perdita, which of course means 'lost', she is instructing him to save her. To find her. Naming her lets her live.

> *Come, poor babe:*
>
> *I have heard, but not believed–*

ROSALIND: *The spirits o' the dead*

> *May walk again.*

WILKINS: Did they do that bit well?

ROSALIND: Yes.

WILKINS: It can really take you away with it, don't you think? When it's done well. Make you forget yourself a little. Your regrets.

> *Beat.*

ROSALIND: *(Quietly acceding.)* Yes. I suppose it can.

WILKINS: *(Finding his footing again.)* My grandfather committed a great number of Shakespeare's plays to memory.

ROSALIND: As did my father!

WILKINS: Really, in their entirety?

ROSALIND: Well, the good ones.

WILKINS: It's so damned impressive. I've always wished I could do the same.

ROSALIND: Then why don't you do it?

WILKINS: *(With levity.)* Oh I don't know. Laziness?

ROSALIND: *(Immediately unimpressed.)* Laziness?

WILKINS: Haven't you heard of it?

ROSALIND: I don't believe in it.

WILKINS: *(Realizing this is true.)*…No. I suppose not.

> *Beat.*

ROSALIND: I'll leave you to it then.

WILKINS: But what are you planning to work on this morning?

ROSALIND: I'll be trying to get an image of DNA that isn't destroyed by the lack of humidity in the camera.

WILKINS: Hm. I suppose we need to fix that problem, don't we.

ROSALIND: *(Taking umbrage.)* Yes. I suppose *we* do.

    Lights shift.

CASPAR: Dear Dr. Franklin.

GOSLING: Don Caspar was a doctoral student in biophysics at Yale. Unlike me, he was actually pretty close to getting his PhD. Not that I was so far off. Or, okay…I was. I don't know why it took me so incredibly long. My mother has her theories but we won't get into those.

CASPAR: My advisor, Simon Dewhurst, recommended I contact you since I'm considering doing the final stage of my doctoral research on the chemical makeup of coal molecules. You are, according to him, the world's expert on the subject. I gather you combine a theoretical and applied approach and this is precisely what I am hoping to do. So, I would be delighted…no…grateful if you would send me some of your scholarship on coal. X-ray images and published articles would be most appreciated.

ROSALIND: Dear Mr. Caspar: Thank you for your letter. Published articles are published and therefore you can access them just as well as I can. It might be possible, however, to send X-ray images so long as you assure me you know how to read them. I would prefer to avoid misinterpretations of my work cropping up all over New Haven. I should like to maintain the reputation your Dr. Dewhurst so kindly attributes to me.

CASPAR: Dear Dr. Franklin, I never received the images in the mail, even though I assured you I understood how to read them. Could you please re-send? It's been over a month and I'm anxious to finalize this section of my dissertation.

    Beat.

Dear Dr. Franklin, I'm so sorry to write again, but I still haven't received the images. I'm afraid I've become a pest. Please forgive me. It would kill me to think you might think badly of me, as I'm such an admirer of your work.

ROSALIND: *(Offhanded.)* Dear Mr. Caspar, I trust you have now received the images?

CASPAR: Dear Dr. Franklin, I have indeed received the images. And I can't thank you enough. They've opened up for me...I mean, you've opened up for me a whole new... What I mean is, I've never seen anything like them. I could stare at them for hours and they still wouldn't reveal all of their secrets. Not that that means I can't read them. I can read them. I just mean that they're beautiful—these shapes within shapes, shapes overlapping, shapes that mean more than what they seem at first glance but are also beautiful simply for what they are. *(A new idea.)* I think one sees something new each time one looks at truly beautiful things.

ROSALIND: *(Formal.)* Thank you, Mr. Caspar. I'm pleased you received the images.

WILKINS: *(Unimpressed.)* One sees something new each time one looks at truly beautiful things?

CASPAR: Yes. I think so. And so did she.

GOSLING: *(To the audience.)* Sometimes she would get away from the lab. I'd arrive in the morning and no one would be there—

WILKINS: *(Hurt/indignant at being overlooked.)* Well, I was there.

GOSLING: And then the telephone would ring.

ROSALIND: *(On the telephone with GOSLING.)* I'm in Switzerland. Switzerland I said.

GOSLING: What? I can't hear you.

ROSALIND: I told you I was going hiking this week-end. I'm just going to stay an extra day.

GOSLING: Fine.

ROSALIND: Can you hear me?

GOSLING: She would just disappear sometimes. One day here and then gone—

WILKINS: Like a restless ghost.

ROSALIND: It's beautiful here, Gosling. You should have smelled the air at the summit; it was—

GOSLING: You have to speak up. I just can't–

ROSALIND: My head feels clear for the first time in ages and I've been doing some really wonderful thinking. I believe I've worked out how to fix the camera. And the Alps seem larger and yet somehow less overwhelming than they have in the past, as though their vastness was made for me, as though the more of something there is to climb, the further I'll get to go. It seems so obvious now. The mountains mean more than what they seem at first glance but are also beautiful simply for what they are…You know, I think one sees something new each time one looks at truly beautiful things.

GOSLING: Miss Franklin? Rosalind? Are you there?

WATSON: *(Unimpressed.)* But she wasn't there, was she. She was too busy snow-shoeing and…enjoying things like…nature and small woodland creatures.

CRICK: I mean, didn't she feel that something was at her back, a force greater than she was…

WATSON: You mean us?

CRICK: No. I mean fate.

WATSON: What's the difference?

WILKINS: And then she'd come back.

ROSALIND: Gosling, more to the left. I said the left.

GOSLING: I am moving it to the left.

ROSALIND: More, you have to move it more. We're simply not aligned.

> *ROSALIND moves into a beam of light.*

GOSLING: Don't step there, Miss Franklin, please!

ROSALIND: Dammit.

GOSLING: You can't move through the beam like that.

ROSALIND: If I have to do everything myself, I will. I mean, don't you understand I will literally go mad if we don't get a better image soon. So let's get it done, Gosling. It's as simple as that.

GOSLING: *(Quietly.)* It doesn't have to be.

ROSALIND: What was that?

GOSLING: I said I'm here to help you. I just don't want to…

ROSALIND: What, Gosling? Don't want to what?

GOSLING: *(To the audience.)* I was going to say "endanger myself" but I didn't. I could have said, "put myself in harm's way," could have said that even though we didn't know it for sure yet, I could feel the way that beam cut through my flesh. Instead I said:

Yesterday's photographs *were* better, the best yet–did you see them?

ROSALIND: Of course I did.

GOSLING: There was a little crowd around them this morning, marveling at them, at the detail you captured.

ROSALIND: *(Feigning disinterest.)* Was there?

GOSLING: Absolutely. They were enthralled.

　　　　Beat.

It's quite gratifying, really. You should feel…

ROSALIND: But they need to be so much clearer, Gosling…If we're ever to find the structure.

GOSLING: I know.

ROSALIND: It's going to get to the heart of everything, Ray.

GOSLING: But you still need to sleep, occasionally. Don't you? Or don't you need any?

ROSALIND: We can call it a night, if you like.

GOSLING: You mean, why don't *I* call it a night?

ROSALIND: *(Smiling to herself.)* They were really enthralled, were they?

GOSLING: Like chickens clucking around a new bit of food.

ROSALIND: Go home, Ray.

GOSLING: So long as you promise not to…

ROSALIND: What?

GOSLING: *(Not brave enough to say what he wants to say.)*...Stay too late. So long as you promise not to stay too late.

ROSALIND: I promise.

GOSLING: You're lying.

ROSALIND: Yes.

CASPAR: *(To GOSLING.)* Did she really do that?

GOSLING: All the time.

CASPAR: And you didn't...

GOSLING: I couldn't...It was like speaking bad French to a French person who insists then on speaking in English just to show you you're not good enough to speak to her in her own language, that she can walk all over you in any language, anywhere.

CASPAR: She did know a lot of languages.

GOSLING: That's not what I meant–

CASPAR: I know.

WILKINS: *(Interrupting.)* Then there was the conference in Naples, spring 1951. And it was typical enough. Everyone pretended to be terribly interested in everyone else's work. My lecture was on the last day and the room was nearly empty. I showed a few slides, explained why we felt DNA was worth studying as opposed to protein, and then packed up my things. I was about to leave but then a young man with really very odd hair blocked my path.

WATSON: I'm Dr. Watson.

WILKINS: Hello, Watson. Can I help you?

WATSON: It's Dr. Watson, but no matter...The thing is, I was fascinated by your presentation.

WILKINS: Well good, thank you.

WATSON: It makes me think–more than ever–that the gene's the thing. I mean, we have to get to the bottom of it–discover how it replicates itself. And so we need its structure. Your slides convinced me that this can and should be done. That the shape is regular enough that it can be studied.

WILKINS: Yes. I believe it is.

WATSON: It's just incredibly exciting.

WILKINS: What is?

WATSON: To be born at the right time. There's an element of fate to it, don't you think? And I don't believe in fate.

WILKINS: You said your name is?

WATSON: *(All confidence and presumption.)* Watson. And I was wondering if maybe I could work with you on nucleic acid? At King's? I don't mean to be presumptuous…

WILKINS: That is a bit…presumptuous. Have we even met before?

WATSON: I'm twenty-two. I already have my doctorate. From Indiana University. I'm currently doing research in Copenhagen on the biochemistry of virus reproduction.

WILKINS: And?

WATSON: What I'm trying to say is: the photographs from your lab are brilliant. I'd like to learn crystallography.

WILKINS: I'm not even positive that I know what we're talking about.

    Beat. A new tactic.

WATSON: *(Matter-of-factly.)* When I was five, my father told me religion was the enemy of progress, a tool used by the rich to give purpose to the lives of the poor.

WILKINS: A rather bold assertion to make to a five year old.

WATSON: He said the *worst* thing is that it eradicates curiosity, because it solves everything. So in my house there was no God. Which meant I needed to go looking for my own set of instructions for life.

WILKINS: *(Not sure where this is going.)* Okay…

WATSON: Which I happened to find in birds.

WILKINS: *(Unimpressed.)* In birds, did you say?

WATSON: My father would take me bird watching. In time, I learned to distinguish two different birds by the tiniest detail. I saw how the males would court the females, singing the most elaborate songs. Sometimes the female joins in and it's a duet. Sometimes he sings only for her.

WILKINS: I'm sorry, but I don't really see the relevance of—

WATSON: *(A little annoyed.)* I saw that the natural world is full of secrets—and no one, least of all me, likes knowing there's a secret without knowing what it is. So I decided I would crack them. Work them all out. The secrets, Maurice—I can call you Maurice, can't I?

WILKINS: Well, no—

WATSON: And the biggest one out there now? The biggest secret? The gene, of course. It's all I can think of. All I see. And I want in on it.

WILKINS: You do, do you.

WATSON: I've gotta get in the race, Wilkins.

WILKINS: What race are you referring to, Watson?

WATSON: For the structure of DNA, obviously.

WILKINS: There is no race.

WATSON: Linus Pauling's on it, out at Caltech.

WILKINS: Well, he doesn't have the sample I have. Or the photographs.

WATSON: Or the photographer.

WILKINS: That's right.

> *WILKINS shuts his briefcase and walks away.*

WATSON: Was it the biggest mistake of his life?

> *Beat, then with glee.*

Without question.

WILKINS: People assume I must feel it *was*—not taking him on, and becoming partners. After all, maybe the two of *us* would have…Maybe later *my* name would have…rolled off the tongue. Been the answer to questions in the occasional pub quiz. I don't know. What happened happened:

WATSON: After our conversation, I approached Lawrence Bragg at the Cavendish, who took me on immediately. I was partnered upon my arrival with a scientist named Francis Crick.

CRICK: Do you prefer Jim, or James? Jim sounds more American to me. Or how about Jimmy?

WATSON: How about I tell you and you don't have to keep guessing.

CRICK: I like that idea.

GOSLING: *(To the audience.)* As a child, already sure he wanted to become a scientist, Crick confessed to his mother that he worried everything would be discovered by the time he grew up. She assured him that this wasn't the case. And from that moment on, he was single-minded…Which is truly impressive. I mean, I don't think I've set my mind to something for more than five minutes in my entire life without wanting then to put the kettle on or to find that letter my brother wrote me three years ago from Wales or to try to remember the song that was playing in the dance hall when that girl walked in who looked like she might almost be willing to talk to me.

Lights shift. Back in the lab.

ROSALIND: Hello, Dr. Wilkins.

WILKINS: Hello Miss Franklin.

ROSALIND: And how was your conference?

WILKINS: I hear from Gosling you're spending some late nights here.

ROSALIND: *(Sharply.)* I'm just doing my work, Dr. Wilkins. Nothing more.

WILKINS: May I see it?

ROSALIND: What?

WILKINS: Your work.

ROSALIND: Why?

WILKINS: We're partners, aren't we, Miss Franklin?

Beat.

Aren't we?

ROSALIND: Yes we are.

WILKINS: So let's have it then.

ROSALIND: For one, I fixed the camera.

WILKINS: The humidity is no longer an issue?

ROSALIND: It's no longer an issue.

WILKINS: How did you do it?

ROSALIND: It was simple, really. I used salt solutions.

WILKINS: And the salt didn't spray the DNA?

ROSALIND: No it didn't. I assured you it wouldn't and it didn't.

WILKINS: Well, I'm very impressed.

ROSALIND: There's no need to condescend.

WILKINS: I wasn't. I am seriously impressed.

ROSALIND: But that's ridiculous. You shouldn't be. I used the simplest of chemist's techniques.

WILKINS: Whatever you did, it was wonderful!

ROSALIND: What's wrong with you, Dr. Wilkins? You look flushed.

WILKINS: I do feel a little warm.

ROSALIND: Maybe you should sit down.

WILKINS: Yes.

He sits, gazing at her. A long beat.

ROSALIND: *(Sharply, awkwardly.)* All right. That should do it. I'm sure you're ready now to get back to work.

WILKINS stands and stares at her, shocked. Lights shift.

WILKINS: But how can we get anything done if she's constantly making me feel as though I'm being impolite to her? No, worse—offensive.

GOSLING: I think she's just settling in.

WILKINS: Did you know Linus Pauling's on DNA now, Gosling?

GOSLING: I didn't.

WILKINS: As I said, we really must push forward.

GOSLING: And we will.

WILKINS: All I've been is kind to her.

GOSLING: *(Warmly.)* So maybe kindness isn't working.

WILKINS: Kindness always works with women, Gosling. I'm a trifle concerned for you if you didn't know that.

>*WILKINS picks up a box of chocolates and enters the lab where GOSLING and ROSALIND are working; her back is to him.*

GOSLING: *(Noticing the chocolates.)* Dr. Wilkins, you shouldn't have.

WILKINS: Oh—no—they're for…

GOSLING: I know who they're for.

ROSALIND: *(Turning around.)* Yes, Wilkins, can I help you?

>*She notices the box.*

What is that?

WILKINS: May I speak with you?

ROSALIND: About what?

WILKINS: Privately.

ROSALIND: Well, all right. But quickly.

>*She nods at GOSLING, who doesn't understand at first.*

GOSLING: Oh, right.

>*He leaves. A beat.*

ROSALIND: So?

WILKINS: I got you these.

He hands her the box.

ROSALIND: What are they?

WILKINS: Chocolates. *(Beat.)* I bought them for you.

ROSALIND: Why?

WILKINS: Why?

ROSALIND: Yes, why?

WILKINS: Oh. I suppose because I think things between us haven't got off on a good foot. On the right foot. I want to…I wanted to…

ROSALIND: We've already started again once, haven't we? How often will we have to do this?

WILKINS: It's just that…I mean, I'd like to…have an easier relationship with you.

ROSALIND: But we're not here to have a relationship, Dr. Wilkins.

WILKINS: *(Turning red.)* I didn't mean a relationship in the, well…I meant a working relationship. An easier partnership.

ROSALIND: Was your wife cold?

WILKINS: I beg your pardon?

ROSALIND: Was she cold?

WILKINS: I don't know what you're…to what you're referring…

ROSALIND: You do, I think. After all, how many wives have you had?

WILKINS: One.

ROSALIND: An American who refused to return with you to England after the birth of your son.

WILKINS: Yes.

ROSALIND: So was she cold?

WILKINS: She could be.

ROSALIND: And I'm not her. We're not married. You don't have to try to win me over. In fact, you shouldn't try to win me over because you won't succeed. I'm not that kind of person.

WILKINS: I'm just trying to…

ROSALIND: What?

WILKINS: Be your friend.

ROSALIND: I don't want to be your friend, Dr. Wilkins.

WILKINS: You don't?

ROSALIND: No.

> *Beat.*

WILKINS: Well then. Enjoy the chocolates.

> *He exits; the lights shift.*

CASPAR: Dear Dr. Franklin, I hope this isn't out of turn, but I wanted to let you know how immensely helpful your images have been. The work is going well. Incredibly well, actually. This morning I realized that for once I *didn't* feel plagued by lack of direction, by this persistent question about what to do with my life and whether I've made the right choices. I have made the right choices. I just love…I mean does the X-ray camera ever seem like it's just an extension of your own eye, as though you and you alone possess the superhuman powers that allow you to see into the heart of things? To understand the nature of the world as though it's a secret no one else is meant to know?…I do. And I think you do too.

ROSALIND: *(All formality.)* Dear Mr. Caspar: Thank you for your letter. And…Yes. I do share some of your…ways of thinking. It's nice to hear that one isn't alone.

GOSLING: And then…then Wilkins gave a lecture and referenced "his" DNA work.

WILKINS: I didn't say it quite like that.

GOSLING: He announced, to great applause, that all the X-ray patterns *he'd* made indicated a clear central x, a helix. And it wasn't pretty–the aftermath, I mean. Not the helix. The helix was…beautiful.

ROSALIND: *(Condescendingly.)* Flushed with pride, are we?

WILKINS: I beg your pardon?

ROSALIND: X-ray patterns *you* made?

WILKINS: It was just a manner of speaking. Everyone knows who's on the team, that there is a team.

ROSALIND: Well, I don't know which X-ray patterns you were looking at, but in the ones I took, it's certainly not clear that there is a helix.

WILKINS: It's like you're unwilling to see it.

ROSALIND: *(Calmly.)* Dr. Wilkins, I was told–before I came to King's–that I would be in charge of X-ray diffraction. Given that, and given the credit you seem bent on grabbing all for yourself, when you deserve none of it, I would suggest, and would certainly prefer, if you went back to optics and your microscopes. A field no one will begrudge you because no one really cares about it.

WILKINS: Why are you doing this?

ROSALIND: I simply don't understand why you would state something, why you would tell a crowd of people, no less, that something is true when it's not.

WILKINS: It might be true!

ROSALIND: It's self-aggrandizement at the cost of any kind of integrity.

WILKINS: You want our funding to continue, don't you? Don't you?

ROSALIND: I'm just not terribly impressed by you is the thing.

WILKINS: Oh?

ROSALIND: You're not…you're just not…you don't command my respect.

WILKINS: That's it.

ROSALIND: I agree. That's it.

WILKINS: No one has ever spoken to me in this way. And I don't deserve it.

ROSALIND: Neither do I!

They part in opposite directions.

GOSLING: Neither did I! Not that that mattered.

The lights shift. ROSALIND is studying two prints.

ROSALIND: Would you look at these, Gosling.

GOSLING peers at the print.

How do you like that? I mean, how do you like that?

GOSLING peers some more.

Well?

GOSLING: What?

ROSALIND: Just look at them, Ray! Jesus.

GOSLING: I see two different X-ray patterns.

ROSALIND: Yes.

GOSLING: One is much more diffuse than the other.

ROSALIND: Yes!

GOSLING: What?

ROSALIND: Don't you see? They're both DNA. It exists in two forms.

CASPAR: A form and B form. The hydrated, longer one was B, and the shorter, wider one, A…It turned out that, before, they'd been looking at one on top of the other, like… well, a man and woman making love, at that point when one body is indistinguishable from the other. It had made them virtually impossible to study. But now Rosalind had discovered how to separate man and woman, how to brush them off, get them out of bed and really see them, naked before her. This achievement alone secured her place in history.

WATSON: *(Scoffing.)* Her place in history?

CRICK: Her place in history??

CASPAR: Well, it should have.

GOSLING: And its significance wasn't lost on Wilkins.

> *ROSALIND and WILKINS work with GOSLING between them.*

WILKINS: Could you please ask Miss Franklin if she would mind terribly if I were to work with her on the A and B forms of DNA. I have some new samples and I think we should collaborate.

GOSLING: Miss Franklin, Dr. Wilkins would like to know if you might consider–

ROSALIND: Please tell him that I will not collaborate and I don't appreciate his desire to infringe on my material.

GOSLING: She says she will not collaborate–

WILKINS: And why is that precisely?

ROSALIND: He knows perfectly well.

GOSLING: She says you know perfectly–

WILKINS: My lord, what's there to be so afraid of??

GOSLING: He says "my lord"–

ROSALIND: I'm not afraid of anything!

GOSLING: She says she's not afraid of anything!

ROSALIND: I mean, I simply will not have my data interpreted for me!

WILKINS: I've really had enough of this.

ROSALIND: I agree.

WILKINS: I mean, I can't take it anymore. What's more, your antipathy is distracting everyone in the lab.

ROSALIND: We'll work separately then. I'll take the A form. And you can have B.

WILKINS: Maybe *I'd* like A.

ROSALIND: Maurice, you're being ridiculous.

WILKINS: Fine. B it is.

CRICK: And so Rosalind did her work. Or tried to. Painstakingly. Paying attention to every detail. Every discrepancy.

WATSON: You see, she was suddenly just a few steps away from the structure. But Rosalind didn't hypothesize the way Crick and I did; she proved things, and proving things, as all scientists know, isn't…well for one thing it isn't fast.

ROSALIND: Either the structure is a big helix or a smaller helix consisting of several chains. The phosphates are also clearly on the outside, and not within.

GOSLING: Did you hear that Linus Pauling's working on DNA again?

ROSALIND: I didn't.

GOSLING: Well, he is.

ROSALIND: Good for him.

GOSLING: I think Wilkins wants to speed things up. Make a model. The others are making models, you know.

ROSALIND: If you'd like to take the day off and build a model, Ray, you're welcome to do so. I'd suggest a train, or an automobile. Those tend to reflect reality fairly well.

CRICK: *(To the audience.)* You see, to Rosalind, making a model was tantamount to negligence. She needed to do all the calculations first, to sit in a dimly lit room and do the maths. So what ended up happening was that she and Wilkins both sat in separate dimly lit rooms, doing maths. Unsurprisingly–

WATSON: Wilkins got lonely.

WILKINS: I wasn't at all lonely.

WATSON: And so he'd visit his old friend Francis Crick in Cambridge. A brilliant new scientist had just joined the lab there too: me.

CRICK: Another pint then?

WILKINS: Oh why not.

CRICK: Yes! Why not. This is practically a celebration! I don't think I've seen you in—what—months now? You've been neglecting me, Maurice.

WILKINS: I know…Tell me what you've been up to. Still on those hemoglobins, Francis?

CRICK: Oh, well, actually—

WATSON: *(Leaping in to change the subject.)* But we're so enjoying hearing about your work.

> *WATSON glares at CRICK to get him to join in.*

CRICK: *(A bit reluctantly.)* It's true…we know all about our own work.

WATSON: There's no fun in that.

WILKINS: It's nice to be here; I must say.

CRICK: She's really that bad?

WILKINS: Worse.

WATSON: The Jews really can be very ornery.

WILKINS: You're telling me.

WATSON: Is she quite overweight?

WILKINS: Why do you ask?

CRICK: James is many things but subtle is not one of them. So you must forgive him, over and over and over again.

WATSON: You don't need to apologize for me, Francis—

CRICK: Oh but I do.

WATSON: All I asked is if—

CRICK: You see, he imagines that she's overweight. The kind of woman who barrels over you with the force of a train.

WATSON: Or a Mack truck.

WILKINS: No, she's not like that. No. She's like…she's like…

> *Lights on ROSALIND somewhere else on the stage; WILKINS gazes at her.*

CASPAR: *(To the audience.)* To Watson and Crick, the shape of something suggested the most detailed analysis of its interior workings. As though, by looking at something you could determine how it came to be…how it gets through each day.

WATSON: Tell us more about these recent photographs.

WILKINS: Well, they're getting clearer. Every day I think I see more, and then I wonder if my mind's playing tricks on me.

WATSON: So you really think it's a helix?

CRICK: Jim—

WILKINS: The thing is, she's keeping me from my own work. And she has all the best equipment, not to mention the best samples. She's hoarding everything.

WATSON: It looks like a helix, Maurice?

WILKINS: What? Oh. Yes. A helix.

CRICK: *(Eliciting a "what are you doing??" glare from Watson.)* Perhaps you should build a model.

WATSON: Well, no need to be hasty about it.

WILKINS: It doesn't matter either way! She's opposed— completely—to models. She doesn't think there's any way they could reflect reality at this point. Mere pointless speculation.

CRICK: *(Trying to help, to nudge WILKINS.)*

But is speculation always pointless?

WILKINS: I think as far as Rosy is concerned.

WATSON: She doesn't sound particularly rosy to me.

CRICK: Does she know you all still call her that behind her back?

WILKINS: Are you joking? She'd have us skinned.

WATSON: I can't wait to meet her.

WILKINS: Oh trust me. You can wait.

GOSLING: He didn't have to wait long. That winter King's held a colloquium on nucleic acid structure. I was the… well, I made coffee at the colloquium. That was my contribution. It was November 1951.

ROSALIND stands in a spotlight, or it's possible that we just hear her lines—a recording, or she speaks from offstage. In this scene, WATSON and CRICK watch her, or watch a space that represents her. Their lines should run over some of hers; they're talking over her.

ROSALIND: As we all know, a nucleic acid is a *macromolecule* composed of chains of monomeric *nucleotides.* This nucleic acid, which I'll shorthand as DNA, exists in two forms. / Let's show that slide.

WATSON: *(To CRICK.)* I wonder how she would look if she took off her glasses and did something novel with her hair.

CRICK: You may be onto something, Watson.

ROSALIND: All right. There it is. / Look closely at it.

WATSON: I mean, she could possibly be attractive if she took even the mildest interest in her clothes. But appearances aside, she is not…engaging.

CRICK: I'll grant you that.

ROSALIND: If you examine it, you can see the transition from A form to B form / in this hydrated sample.

WATSON: When we shook hands, her handshake was far too firm. There's nothing gentle, nothing remotely tender about her. She's a cipher where a woman should be. That said, she's not fat.

GOSLING: So busy analyzing the speaker, they didn't hear what she was saying. That she stated quite clearly that:

ROSALIND: Based on these calculations, we can be sure that the phosphates exist on the *outside* of the molecule. There is no question that this is the case.

GOSLING: And when Watson and Crick made their model a week or so later, everyone at King's was invited up to see it—after all, it was based on *our* work.

WATSON: Wilkins, what do you make of it?

ROSALIND: Where's the water?

CRICK: It's nice to see you too, Miss Franklin.

ROSALIND: DNA absorbs at least ten times more water than that.

WATSON: Is that right?

ROSALIND: I don't see how a molecule, if it's as you've imagined it, could hold together.

CRICK: How so?

ROSALIND: The phosphates have to be on the outside. Furthermore, the X-ray data has not proven that the molecule is, indeed, helical.

WATSON: You just don't want to admit that it's right.

WILKINS: It's not right, Watson. It would never hold together. Not like that. Perhaps if you'd told me what you were working on a few weeks ago I could have helped you with it.

CRICK: All right, old boy–

WILKINS: But you didn't do that, did you? And why not? Because you knew perfectly well it wasn't yours to ask about.

WATSON: Maurice–

CRICK: Be quiet, Jim. He's right–we should have told him.

WATSON: Why? It's a free country, isn't it?

CRICK: England? No, not in the slightest.

WATSON: Even if the model *is* wrong–I don't really see what the big deal is.

WILKINS: Then perhaps you should return to *your* country, where theft and burglary are upheld as virtues. In fact, it's how America came to be, isn't it? In Britain we don't actually believe in turning our sinners into saints.

WATSON: Hey, if you're angry with George Washington, don't take it out on me. I'm just trying to do some science here.

ROSALIND: You call that science?

WILKINS: Well you're not trying in the right way…And you're too young. And your hair…needs attention!

WATSON: I'm not too young.

CRICK: For my part I quite like his hair! I think it's got character!

CASPAR: It was a disaster. An embarrassment. The model, I mean. The Cavendish ordered Watson and Crick to stop working on DNA.

WILKINS: An oddly satisfying disaster, wouldn't you say, Ray?

GOSLING: I would, Dr. Wilkins. It was oddly satisfying.

CRICK: What bastards those King's boys can be, can't they? The way they condescended to us.

WATSON: Boys and *girl.*

CRICK: Right. I don't know how he puts up with her. They make quite a pair. I mean I love him dearly, I do, but even at university, Wilkins could be a patronizing prat.

WATSON: Oh come on. We'd be gloating too. If it'd been the reverse.

CRICK: It will be, one day. There's not a chance I'm going back to hemoglobin diffraction patterns.

WATSON: I don't blame you.

Lights shift. ROSALIND is on the telephone.

ROSALIND: You really don't have to worry about me, mother. I'm just fine. I always have been and nothing is different now…
Well, tell father the work is slow-going but…
Of course he's busy, so am I…
Yes: I am managing to sleep…
No. I'm not too lonely.

From offstage.

GOSLING: Miss Franklin!

ROSALIND: I've got to go. Yes. Friday night. Goodbye.

GOSLING: Miss Franklin!

She hangs up. GOSLING appears.

ROSALIND: What is it?

GOSLING: You just have to see it. It's sort of…well, amazing.

ROSALIND: Show me.

He shows her. She studies it for a long time.

ROSALIND: Gosling.

GOSLING: It's incredible, isn't it?

ROSALIND: How do you like that. How do you like that…I've never seen anything like it.

CASPAR: Photograph 51.

WATSON: Photograph 51.

GOSLING: It's certainly a helix. The B form is certainly a helix.

A beat.

ROSALIND: The B form certainly *looks to be* a helix.

GOSLING: Looks to be?

ROSALIND: *(To the audience.)* As a girl, I prided myself on always being right. Because I *was* always right. I drove my family near mad by relentlessly proposing games to play that I'd win every time. Scrabble. Ludo. Hide and Seek outside until the lamplighter appeared on his bicycle and our mother called us in, out of the dusk. Eventually and unsurprisingly I lost my opponents. And when I was at university, and it was becoming as clear to my parents as it always had been for me that I would pursue science, I left Cambridge to meet my father for a hiking weekend. Atop a mountain in the Lake District, when I was eighteen-years old, he said to me, "Rosalind, if you go forward with this life…you must never be wrong. In one instance, you could lose all you've achieved." But I didn't think this would be a problem. I was meticulous and I enjoyed being meticulous because I enjoyed being right. But it was in that moment that, without realizing it, a kind of fear set in, a dread around the edges of my convictions, like a hovering dusk no lamplighter ever truly dispels.

She looks again at the photograph, intently.

CASPAR: And she stood there, staring at the photograph, as though she were looking in a mirror but was suddenly unrecognizable to herself.

CRICK: *(Searchingly.)* Did any chimes go off in her head? Was there any singing?

WATSON: And then.

She opens a drawer and files it away.

WATSON: *(Shocked.)* She put it away.

GOSLING: Shouldn't we show it to Wilkins?

ROSALIND: Don't you want to celebrate, Gosling? We should celebrate.

WILKINS entering.

WILKINS: Celebrate what? I see no cause for celebration.

ROSALIND: You can have a little fun, can't you, Maurice? After all, we know how you like your games and jokes and things.

WILKINS: Do I?

ROSALIND: Why don't you give us a little speech.

WILKINS: I beg your pardon?

ROSALIND: Go on then.

WILKINS: A speech? About what?

ROSALIND: Be creative, Maurice. You can do that. Come up with something out of thin air. Can't you?...I don't know. Why don't you tell us about the fondest moment in your scientific career.

WILKINS: The fondest moment.

ROSALIND: Ray, does it seem he's just repeating after me?

GOSLING: Oh, um.

WILKINS: What is it precisely you want me to do?

ROSALIND: Just do *something*. Maurice. Something. You never commit to anything and it torments me.

WILKINS: Does it.

ROSALIND: Yes. I can't abide it.

GOSLING: I think Dr. Wilkins is just trying to…

ROSALIND: Oh, come on, Ray. Whose side are you on?

GOSLING: *(Directing the first phrase to ROSALIND and the second to WILKINS in quick, seamless succession.)* I'm not on a side. I'm not on a side.

WILKINS: You're behaving a bit like a banshee, Miss Franklin.

ROSALIND: Just celebrate with us.

WILKINS: But what are we celebrating??

GOSLING: It's amazing, really—

ROSALIND: Have some faith in me. There is something to celebrate. Take a leap of faith.

WILKINS: *(Bitterly.)* As though you would ever do that.

>*He chuckles, drily.*

I mean, my God, can you even hear yourself? The irony?

ROSALIND: *(Slowly.)* I take a leap of faith every day, Maurice, just by walking through that door in the morning. I take a leap of faith that it'll all be worth it, that it will all ultimately mean something.

WILKINS: I don't know what you're talking about.

ROSALIND: No, you wouldn't.

WILKINS: You know, you really are unspeakably difficult. I've never encountered a woman with such temerity—

ROSALIND: Well perhaps it's that you haven't encountered very many women.

WILKINS: As you well know I was married!

ROSALIND: And maybe that's over and done with for a reason.

WILKINS: Oh, no. No. I refuse to get into this with you—

GOSLING: Dr. Wilkins—

WILKINS: *(Bitter and sarcastic and self-pitying, a dam bursting.)* No. I refuse to disclose the depths of my wife's cruelties to you. The lengths she took to keep me from our son; the words she said that repeat over and over in my head, like an infernal radio show that will never end. I will not get into it. I am not that kind of man. Perhaps you want to work with someone different. Someone who can happily remain in high dudgeon with you day in and day out. Well, I'm sorry—I am not that person. I'm sorry! Life is and has always been unfair. *That* is its enduring hallmark.

ROSALIND: Maurice—

WILKINS: A leap of faith. It's almost funny…Because *you* would never. No—it all has to be solved and re-solved. There can be no room for error. No room for…humanity, really. That's what you leave out of *your* equations, Miss Franklin.

    He leaves.

GOSLING: That night I slipped Wilkins the photograph. I did think it was his right to see it. I knew it was the best photograph we had.

CASPAR: Dr. Franklin, I graduated today!! As of this morning, I was still a student, and a mere few hours later, I'm not. I feel like one of my own X-ray exposures, one that took ages to set up and wasn't at all promising, but managed to yield something. A little something. Really, I can't believe it. Neither could my parents. They kept saying "Don, we thought you'd never finish." But they were happy. And…I was happy—am happy—and I just felt like telling you that I owe all of this to you. And I was wondering…do you think…I mean, is there any chance I could come work with you—for you—at King's? It would be a great honor. Maybe there's a fellowship I could look into?

ROSALIND: Dear *Dr.* Caspar, my most heartfelt congratulations. I'm sure you realize how important semantics are. This title that's now been conferred on you…It means windows have been flung wide, letting in the cold night air, that streetlamps will blink on as you walk past them. In 1945, when I got my doctorate, I thought those letters you've now acquired would have the same value for me, but of course you and I well know this is not the case. I'm not complaining about it. One can't focus on such things. And I don't.

CASPAR: You are so remarkable, Dr. Franklin. I really hope you don't mind my saying: you are so remarkable. I don't know how you exist in the environment in which you find yourself.

ROSALIND: I just do my work, Dr. Caspar. I've realized the best thing is just to do one's work and not worry so much about anything else. It doesn't matter anyway.

WATSON: But it does matter! It did matter. You can't be in the race and ignore it at the same time! That's where she went wrong.

WILKINS: You told her she was remarkable?

CASPAR: I did.

CRICK: And what is a race anyway? And who wins? If life is the ultimate race to the finish line, then really we don't *want* to win it. Shouldn't *want* to win it. Should we?

WATSON: I don't know what you're talking about. Sometimes you didn't make sense, Francis, and I had to pretend to understand what you were saying. I usually attributed it to a British thing, some guilty remnant of an imperialist past back to haunt you.

CRICK: Or maybe the race is for something else entirely. Maybe none of us really knew what we were searching for. What we wanted. Maybe success is as illusory and elusive as…well, Rosalind was to us. Maybe it exists only in our conception of it, and then always just out of reach, like Tantalus with his hovering grapes.

WATSON: See? Gobble-de-gook. It's amazing we got on so well for so long.

CRICK: *(Sarcastic.)* It is amazing.

> *Then, softening. The tension breaks and they smile at each other.*

WATSON: In January 1953 we got our hands on a report Pauling had written about nucleic acid structure. It was wrong; he was wrong about the phosphates, but the simple fact of his writing it meant he was working on it in earnest, which meant he would get it.

CRICK: We all knew it was just a matter of time and not much time at that. So Watson went to London. He didn't tell me why, but I had a feeling.

WATSON bursts into ROSALIND's office.

WATSON: Good morning, good morning, lovely Rosalind.

ROSALIND: What are you doing here?

WATSON: It's nice to see you too.

ROSALIND: You could knock.

WATSON: Do you know what I have with me?

ROSALIND: How would I know?

WATSON: Pauling's manuscript.

ROSALIND: All right.

WATSON: All right?

ROSALIND: Look, I really was about to–

WATSON: Pauling is going to be publicly humiliated in two weeks when this gets published and you don't even want to see it?

ROSALIND: Why would I want to see it?

WATSON: To gloat, for one. You should see Bragg—he's walking on water these days; *(Impersonating Bragg.)* "Linus isn't going to beat me this time!" See, Pauling made some of the same mistakes Crick and I made. He's proposing a triple-stranded helix with the phosphates on the inside.

ROSALIND: That's what this rush to publish does. It means our publications are littered with ridiculous mistakes.

WATSON: Do you think DNA is a helix?

ROSALIND: I'm happy to arrange a time to sit down with you and discuss my findings but right now is not possible, unfortunately.

WATSON: Maurice says you're anti-helical.

ROSALIND: Maurice has no business saying who or what I am.

WATSON: So you think it is helical?

ROSALIND: I think it might be.

WATSON: Are you sure you're interpreting your data correctly?

ROSALIND: What did you just say?

WATSON: How much theory do you have?

A hair of a beat.

ROSALIND: Why are you here, Jim?

WATSON: *(Holding up PAULING's manuscript.)* To share.

ROSALIND: Oh, really?

Beat.

WATSON: I don't know. I thought you'd be interested in the manuscript. I thought…

ROSALIND: Yes?

WATSON: I thought we could talk.

ROSALIND: But you've never shown any interest in doing that before. Which leads me to believe that you're here to insult me. That or you're not aware of the fact that you're insulting me, which is, perhaps, worse. Do you think that if you demoralize me I won't get it done?

WATSON: Get what done?

ROSALIND: The work, Jim.

WATSON: I think you'll get it done. Or…I think you might get it done. But to do that, you have to compensate for the things you're lacking. And maybe I could do that.

ROSALIND: Do what?

WATSON: Help you.

ROSALIND: Really, if you wouldn't mind leaving–

WATSON: What I mean is, if you had theory you might understand how these "anti-helical" features in the A form are really distortions. That what you're seeing is, in fact, a helix. Because I really think it is one, Rosalind. I have this feeling that's divorced from reason. That I can't explain.

It's deeper than…I mean, if I've known anything for sure in my life, this is it.

ROSALIND: You must sleep so easily. With that kind of certainty.

WATSON: No. I don't sleep.

    Beat.

There's too much to think about. You know there is. It overwhelms you. I can see that. So share your research with me. I mean, you're not going to get it on your own.

ROSALIND: Get out.

WATSON: Be reasonable, Rosalind.

ROSALIND: Get out of my lab!

WATSON: There's no need to get so upset–

ROSALIND: I'm not upset! I'm not upset. I'm…I'm…What I am is none of your concern. Just go.

WATSON: Why won't you even consider that–

    ROSALIND rushes at him.

What's this all about?

ROSALIND: Out!

WATSON: Okay, okay.

    He leaves.

ROSALIND: And stay out.

CASPAR: Down the hall, Watson was with Wilkins. Or Wilkins was with Watson. If it weren't in poor taste, they'd have been holding hands.

WILKINS: Don't be absurd.

CASPAR: I wasn't.

WATSON: She really is a right old hag, isn't she? I mean, the way she lunged at me. I really thought I might get hit.

WILKINS: A complete disaster. Did it to me once. All I was doing was trying to be congenial.

WATSON: Me too!

WILKINS: She takes everything so seriously.

WATSON: One needs to be more lighthearted sometimes. Every now and then at least.

WILKINS: I know.

WATSON: I mean, I can't believe this is what you've had to put up with. It's really more than anyone should be asked to do.

WILKINS: It really is.

WATSON: It is.

WILKINS: And it's all such a shame.

WATSON: What is?

WILKINS: That we're not actually partners. I suppose I ruined that before it even began.

WATSON: How could you have ruined it?

WILKINS: I was unfriendly, I suppose.

WATSON: *(Lying.)* Come on. You're one of the…friendliest men I know.

WILKINS: I know! I mean, I am pretty friendly. I've never offended anyone else.

WATSON: She must be crazy.

WILKINS: Maybe she is. Or maybe…

WATSON: What?

WILKINS: I don't know.

WATSON: Well, you're better off without her. Why collaborate with someone with whom it's impossible to get along?

WILKINS: The work, for one! I mean, you should see some of her…

> *He looks through a file in a drawer and pulls out a photograph.*

This photograph she took of B, for instance.

WATSON: What photograph?

WILKINS: This one.

He hands it to WATSON, who studies it for a long time.

WATSON: I need to…

WILKINS: What?

WATSON: Go. I need to go.

WILKINS: Just like that?

WATSON is out the door.

James?

CASPAR: In *The Double Helix*, Watson later wrote "The instant I saw the picture my mouth fell open and my pulse began to race." It was Photograph 51.

WILKINS: You can't leave–just like that. James!

GOSLING: On the train back to Cambridge, he sketched the image in the margin of a newspaper. He stared at it. He stared at it some more. When the train pulled in, he stopped for a moment to notice two warblers perched atop a station lamppost; he was sure he heard their song as he ran like a wild man down the rainy streets–and then he arrived.

CRICK: What is it?

WATSON: The Nobel.

CRICK: What?

WATSON: The answer.

CRICK: What's the answer?

WATSON: It's a double helix. I saw it.

CRICK: Where?

WATSON: At King's. And we have to build another model. Right now. We have to start right now. We've got it, Francis. It's ours. They're sitting on it and they don't know it. It's ours. This is how we're gonna get to replication.

CRICK: But I don't quite understand.

WATSON: There's no time to understand. We just have to start.

CRICK: Well, let me at least finish this cup of tea. It's really such a lovely cup of tea –

WATSON: Francis!

CRICK: Oh, all right.

WILKINS: But that's not how it happened. I didn't just give him the photograph. He asked for it.

WATSON: No. I don't think so. You offered it up, like a leg of lamb we'd share for dinner.

WILKINS: I didn't.

GOSLING: And that same week–

WILKINS: *(Unhappily.)* Don Caspar arrived.

GOSLING: Shortly after getting his doctorate, Dr. Caspar was awarded a fellowship with us at King's. Apparently, one of the scientists here had gone to bat for him, so to speak. I can't imagine who it was.

The lights shift. WILKINS shepherds CASPAR into the lab.

WILKINS: And this is Miss Franklin.

CASPAR: You're Dr. Franklin?

ROSALIND: That's me.

CASPAR: Well, hello.

An awkward beat. WILKINS looks on, stunned.

It's funny…I imagined you differently.

ROSALIND: How did you imagine me?

CRICK: He didn't say–he couldn't say–that he'd imagined her dowdier. A woman whose exterior mirrored her seriousness.

CASPAR: Oh, just fairer maybe. Blonde.

ROSALIND: You thought I was blonde?

CASPAR: I don't know. Yes.

ROSALIND: You knew I was Jewish, though?

CASPAR: Yes. So am I.

ROSALIND: That will make two of us at King's.

CASPAR: I have left the States, haven't I.

ROSALIND: Yes. I suppose you have…And how was your journey?

WILKINS: His journey was fine—so, shall we?

CASPAR: It was fine. A little tiring.

ROSALIND: Yes—it must have been.

>   *Beat.*

CASPAR: It's strange to meet someone with whom one has—

ROSALIND: We should get to work then, shouldn't we?

WILKINS: Yes. I think work is the reason why we're all here, isn't it? Isn't it, Miss Franklin.

ROSALIND: It certainly is Dr. Wilkins.

GOSLING: Four days later Crick invited Wilkins for Sunday lunch in Cambridge. He found, when he arrived –

CRICK: I hope you don't mind that I invited Watson too.

WILKINS: No, of course not.

CRICK: What can I get you to drink? Odile is making a roast but it won't be ready for an hour or so.

WILKINS: Anything is fine. Whiskey?

CRICK: Whiskey it is.

>   *CRICK exits.*

WATSON: So how has it been lately with you-know-who?

WILKINS: Don't ask.

WATSON: She's working hard?

WILKINS: Same as always…

WATSON: People never change, do they.

WILKINS: No…And I wonder sometimes if perhaps I shouldn't move—you know, to the countryside. I can't really…That is to say, I haven't met anyone in London.

Have you met anyone out here? I mean…I suppose I mean…women? Do you meet women?

CRICK returns with a drink.

CRICK: One whiskey.

WATSON: I have met a few women here. Sure.

CRICK: "Met" being the operative word. They take one look at him and then…how would one describe it…I suppose then there's a brief period of whispering after which time they end up leaving the pub because one turns out to have left her hat at home or some such nonsense. No, it's more likely James would solve the secret of life than bed a woman.

WATSON: Now why d'you say that? It's just none of the women here happen to appreciate my sophisticated charms.

WILKINS: Francis, do you remember Margaret Ramsay?

CRICK: You think I could forget Margaret Ramsay?

WILKINS: *(To WATSON.)* She was–

CRICK: One of the very few women in science at Cambridge. And he was absolutely smitten by her. And then one night they were sitting at opposite ends of his room, talking about the typical things one talked about, I suppose–and out of nowhere he tells her he's in love with her. The poor sod doesn't take her out, get a few drinks in her and kiss her. No he tells her he's fallen for her and then continues to sit there, waiting for some verbal reciprocation of his love.

WATSON: And what happened?

WILKINS: After a very long silence, she stood, said goodbye and left.

CRICK: See, women expect men to fall upon them like unrestrained beasts. Despite their murmurings to the contrary, they want to feel that you can't keep your hands off them. Maurice has never understood that.

WILKINS: I suppose what I'm wondering is…how do you and Odile…how does it work so well?

WATSON: It works because she doesn't know that he ogles every other woman who crosses his path.

CRICK: I don't! I mean, give me some credit. Sometimes I do much more than ogle.

WILKINS: But you love her?

WATSON: What is this? Twenty Questions?

CRICK: Of course I love her. I mean, honestly I don't know what I'd do without her. I can't even imagine that life. And as soon as we have the money, we're going to have gads of children…

WATSON: *(In horror.)* God, how many is that?

CRICK: Well, at least one.

> *He laughs but WILKINS looks away, sad.*

CRICK: *(Studying WILKINS.)*

What is it, Maurice? Is something wrong?

> *Beat.*

WILKINS: Oh, it's…I don't know. It's just that I'm starting to think there might come a point in life after which one can't really begin again.

WATSON: That's right. It's called birth. After that point, what's done is done. Which leads us nicely to a discussion of genes. So shall we discuss how the work is going?

WILKINS: *(With sarcasm.)* Yes, the work, the work. That is the important thing, isn't it?

WATSON: Do tell us what our little ray of sunshine is keeping busy with these days.

CRICK: *(Actually worried.)* Wilkins, old boy. Are you sure you're quite all right?

WATSON: Anything new on her docket? If you don't mind sharing, that is.

WILKINS: I honestly couldn't give two damns. I'm happy to tell you all I can remember.

WATSON: Well–good. Isn't that good, Crick?

CRICK: *(Reluctantly.)* Yes–it's good.

> *Beat. And a decision to go along with the change of topic.*

WILKINS: So let's see…She's writing a paper at the minute. She might never finish it. The woman writes so slowly to begin with and lately she's been a bit distracted. Infuriating, really.

WATSON: What's it on then?

WILKINS: Her recent photographs, I'm sure. As you saw, they were the best yet.

WATSON: *(Tossed off.)* Yes. They were good. Very good.

And is she building a model?

WILKINS: Starting to entertain the idea. Which is actually something.

WATSON: Is she? I didn't know that. Francis, did you know that?

CRICK: I didn't know that, Jim.

WILKINS: She has so much information now she can no longer completely avoid it.

WATSON: What kind of model would she make?

WILKINS: One of B. It turns out A is no longer viable on its own. So essentially A *and* B have become hers. I'm not quite sure how that happened, but it happened. And yes, a model may come out of it. Someday.

CRICK: Oh, well good.

WATSON: That's terrific for her. *(Beat.)* We wish her well.

CRICK: Yes.

WILKINS: *(Shocked.)* You do??

WATSON: Of course.

CRICK: But how would you feel, Maurice, if…

WILKINS: What?

CRICK: I mean…what it is I mean to say is–

WATSON: He wonders if you'd be opposed to our trying. One more time. To get at the thing.

WILKINS: You want to build another model?

CRICK: Would that be all right with you?

WATSON: We wanted to ask you first. This time. Since it really is your...thing.

GOSLING: They neglected to mention that they'd already begun.

CRICK: You really should get to it yourself, old boy. You can do one too.

WATSON: It's a super idea. You do one too.

WILKINS: I can't do one. Not with Rosy around. It's her territory, her materials...

CRICK: So that's grand. You'll do it if Rosy ever leaves.

WATSON: Yes, grand! She's bound to go sometime, after all.

CRICK: And we'll get started on ours, so long as you give us the go-ahead.

WILKINS: I can't tell you what to do. I just...

WATSON: Yes?

WILKINS: I didn't know you were interested is all. In doing it yourselves. Not again. Not after what happened last time around. I mean, weren't you sufficiently embarrassed?

WATSON: Maurice, if I hid out after every embarrassment, I'd probably never be able to leave my room.

CRICK: And his room is an embarrassment. Utterly filthy. Why do you think he's here all the time?

WATSON: Odile's roasts aren't bad.

CRICK: You take that back. They're superb.

WATSON: Almost as tender as her thighs.

CRICK: Okay, that's enough.

WILKINS: Look, if I'd known you were going to do another, I wouldn't have...

CRICK: What, Maurice?

WILKINS: Said so much, I suppose. Or shown you…

GOSLING: Then things moved quickly. Quickly especially by the standards of a PhD student for whom everything moves slowly.

CASPAR: Watson and Crick got hold of the paper Rosalind had written. It was confidential.

CRICK: It wasn't confidential. Another scientist at Cambridge gave it to us after it was circulated to a committee over which he was presiding.

WILKINS: Well it wasn't published, that's for sure. And it included her latest calculations, confirmation that the B-form was helical, and the diameter of that helix. Information that became critical to your work.

WATSON: I'm sure we would have gotten there sooner or later, even without it.

WILKINS: So would we have done, with the benefit of your work. You had ours but we didn't have yours!

WATSON: There was no "we" where you were concerned. That was the problem.

GOSLING: Anyway, it doesn't matter how they got the paper, only that they got it.

CASPAR: And that Rosalind didn't know she should be in a hurry. Neither of us knew.

> *CASPAR is leaning over a microscope and ROSALIND tries to squeeze by him.*

ROSALIND: Would you excuse me, Dr. Casp–

> *She brushes against him, just a little.*

Oh I'm sorry.

CASPAR: *(Straightening.)* It's fine.

ROSALIND: I was just…

CASPAR: It's fine, Rosalind.

> *Beat.*

ROSALIND: *(Taking offense.)* What's happened? You got your degree and somehow I lost mine?

CASPAR: I'm sorry—*Dr.* Franklin…It's just.

ROSALIND: What?

CASPAR: I like your name…Rosalind…Rosy.

ROSALIND: Why?

CASPAR: It's warm. It makes me think about coming inside to a fire after a walk in the bitter cold.

WILKINS: *(To the audience.)* Only an American could come up with such a line.

ROSALIND: But I'm not warm. No one thinks I'm warm. Ask anyone—

CASPAR: Listen…

ROSALIND: Yes?

CASPAR: Would you have dinner with me?

ROSALIND: Dinner??

CASPAR: No—not like…Just dinner…Something really casual.

ROSALIND: I don't think you understand that nothing in Britain is casual. No—everything here is filled with meaning no one will name or indulge. It's why I much preferred Paris.

CASPAR: But I would think it must have been very hard to be in Paris.

ROSALIND: Why's that?

CASPAR: I don't know. After the war. It must not have been too friendly to…

ROSALIND: Oh. Yes. But…you just have to get by, don't you? That's all one can do. You can't constantly be thinking about that…or I imagine it would destroy you.

CASPAR: It would. I'm certain it would.

> *Beat.*

Have dinner with me.

Beat.

ROSALIND: I'm afraid there just isn't time, Dr. Caspar.

CASPAR: For dinner?

ROSALIND: Right.

GOSLING: In the meantime, Watson and Crick were working at breakneck speed.

CASPAR: After looking at Rosalind's report, they made a conclusion she had yet to draw: that DNA consisted of *two* chains running in opposite directions, a pair of endless spirals that work together but will never meet.

CRICK: Which will lead us to how it replicates, Watson. To how it all works.
...Do you know what this means?

WATSON: Yes. I mean, no.

CRICK: It means large homes in the countryside without leaky radiators. It means suits tailored to fit. It means my mother will stop politely asking why I didn't go into law, or medicine, and whether I have any regrets about the way my life has turned out...

WATSON: It means textbook publishers will call to make sure they have the correct spelling of our names.

CRICK: Yes! And you can choose any woman as your wife. And my wife will look at me differently.

WATSON: It means there will always be the means to keep doing this. Forever.

CRICK: We're almost there, Watson. We're so close.

GOSLING: Mid-February. Watson and Crick were all of a sudden being very friendly. They invited everyone to Cambridge—well, everyone except me—and then acted... strangely cheerful.

CRICK: Rosalind! So good to see you! Come in, come in—here, let me take your coat.

WATSON: You're looking particularly lovely today, particularly vibrant—

ROSALIND: Hello Jim. Francis. *(Beat.)* Maurice.

CRICK: And you must be Dr. Caspar.

CASPAR: Please—call me Don.

ROSALIND: Now what was so important that we come all the way here?

CRICK: Just the pleasure of your company, Miss Franklin, on a lovely winter's day. Nothing more.

WATSON: Why not wait out the winter doldrums together? By a warm fire, maybe, sipping the finest Cambridge has to offer.

ROSALIND: You'd be silly to waste a day like this indoors. And I certainly won't, not after being cooped up on the train all morning. Will you come with me to the garden...Don?

CASPAR: Of course...Rosalind.

> *WILKINS watches her take CASPAR's arm; the two exit together.*

WILKINS: She's different.

WATSON: Not to me. Still the same old—

CRICK: Come now. Let's be kind.

WILKINS: *I've* always been kind to her! I've been nothing but kind!

> *He leaves them standing there.*

CRICK: Oh.

WATSON: What was *that?*

CRICK: Ohhhhhhhhh.

WATSON: What??

CRICK: Don't you see?

WATSON: See what?

CRICK: Sometimes you can be so blind, Jim.

WATSON: I can be blind? That's a funny notion.

CRICK: He's in love with her.

WATSON: In love with who?

> *Beat.*

No!!

CRICK: Undeniably.

WATSON: That's quite a theory, Francis. But do you have any proof?

CRICK: That's not the way we work, now. Is it.

> *ROSALIND and CASPAR come back inside. WILKINS is watching them.*

ROSALIND: Francis—Dr. Casp—I mean, Don—just had the most fascinating idea—

WATSON: Oh yes? About what exactly? About helices, or?

ROSALIND: He was proposing that isomorphous replacement could be used with the Tobacco Mosaic Virus.

WILKINS: It's not so novel.

CRICK: No, it's a first class idea.

WATSON: So you'd put atoms of—

CASPAR: Lead, or maybe mercury—something heavy—

CRICK: Into the virus protein to see what the difference would be between the X-ray patterns. The X-ray with the atoms and the one without. That would determine the structure. It's very clever.

CASPAR: Soon enough we'll be making a model, right, Rosy?

WILKINS: She doesn't like being called Rosy.

> *An awkward pause.*

ROSALIND: *(Quietly.)* I don't mind it.

WILKINS: And she doesn't like making models!

> *Awkward silence.*

WATSON: But are you thinking of making one?

> *CRICK breaks in to stop WATSON from going on.*

CRICK: And how much longer will you be in London, Caspar?

CASPAR: Not very much longer, I'm afraid. This fellowship is just a couple more months.

CRICK: Shame.

CASPAR: It is.

They all look at ROSALIND.

ROSALIND: Yes. *(Beat.)* Shame.

WILKINS: *(With unconcealed glee.)* Quite a shame. Yes.

WATSON: Wilkins, you old rogue.

WILKINS: What?

WATSON: Francis, I do believe you're right.

WILKINS: Right about what?

CRICK: Let's move into the sitting room, shall we? Jim, you go and help Odile bring out our new tea set and then we'll sit and have a nice cup.

WATSON: Why should I help her? She's *your* wife.

CRICK: Just go.

Lights shift.

CASPAR: But don't be fooled. She was not distracted by me. Rosalind? No. She continued to work slowly and methodically, and in increasing isolation.

GOSLING: Can I get you anything? A cup of tea at least?

ROSALIND: Gosling, if I were to tell you that it seemed to me the A form of DNA is *not* helical, what would you say?

GOSLING: I'd say you're testing me.

ROSALIND: How so.

GOSLING: Because if the A form is not helical, then neither can the B form be helical, and yet we are confident that it is.

ROSALIND: Yes.

GOSLING: So you were testing me.

ROSALIND: You always need to rule out the wrong answer, Ray. Don't forget that.

GOSLING: So then what's the right answer?

ROSALIND: What is the right answer.

GOSLING: Are you asking me?

ROSALIND: Do you know it?

GOSLING: No.

ROSALIND: Then I'm not asking.

CASPAR: Watson and Crick struggled with how the four bases fit into the picture. Did they pair up? Work together? Or were they distinct from each other?

WATSON: You can't be tired. Are you really tired?

CRICK: No. I'm wide awake. I'm just feigning fatigue to keep you on your toes.

WATSON: Are you kidding? I can't tell if you're kidding.

CRICK: I can't tell either.

GOSLING: February the 23rd.

> *ROSALIND is studying prints of the A and B forms. She holds them very far away from her face and then very close.*

ROSALIND: Gosling! Can you come here, Gosling.

GOSLING: What is it?

ROSALIND: What are you doing over there, playing solitaire?

GOSLING: No, I was just–

ROSALIND: What do you think this is? Nursery school? I mean, we have work to do.

GOSLING: But you haven't been wanting my help–

ROSALIND: Please just stand here, will you. *(Beat.)* No–that's too close. Still a little further. I need you to be standing further away so I can think.

> *She picks up the photograph again, studies it.*

Yes. Both the A and B form are helical. They have to be.

GOSLING: Two steps away from the solution. Two steps away. She just didn't know it.

WILKINS entering.

WILKINS: It's late. Why don't you go home.

ROSALIND: I'm fine.

WILKINS: Fine.

He begins to leave. She is staring at Photograph 51.

You're staring. I can tell you're doing nothing more than staring. Go home.

ROSALIND: No.

WILKINS: Or let me look at it.

He goes towards her.

Is it the bases? Are you thinking about the bases?

ROSALIND: I think I'm thinking about how I've come to the end of thinking. How there's nothing left.

WILKINS: You're exhausted.

ROSALIND: Not exhausted. Blank.

WILKINS: This rarely happens to you.

ROSALIND: It never happens.

WILKINS: Never?

Beat.

You think if you gave an inch, we'd all take a mile, is that it?

ROSALIND: *(Quietly.)* It's true, isn't it?

WILKINS: No. I don't think so.

ROSALIND: Then you too have come to the end of thought. You should go home, Maurice.

WILKINS: I could…

ROSALIND: What?

WILKINS: We could talk it through. It might help.

A long beat. She stares at WILKINS.

GOSLING: For a moment, everything stopped. Different ways our lives could go hovered in the air around us.

A long beat.

ROSALIND: You know, I think I *am* going to call it a night. I haven't been home before midnight for a fortnight and really what's the point of being here and not getting anywhere?

She stands abruptly.

GOSLING: And then there was only one way everything would go.

ROSALIND: Goodnight, Maurice.

She exits.

WILKINS: Goodnight.

GOSLING: February the 28th, 1953. A barmaid made her way through the Cambridge snow to open the Eagle Pub for the day. Watson and Crick were holed up like birds in a cage that was about to become…the world.

WATSON: They must pair off. The hydrogen bonds form between the pairs.

CRICK: Adenine always goes with thymine; cytosine with guanine.

WATSON: Whenever there's one on the DNA chain, there's always the other.

CRICK: Yes!

WILKINS: Like a team. A successful team.

GOSLING: And in the meantime, in a quiet Italian restaurant overlooking the Thames, where waiters stay out of people's way, Rosalind wondered if she was on a date. She couldn't be sure. She'd never been on one before.

> *ROSALIND and CASPAR sit at a table together. It's the end of the meal.*

CASPAR: I'm glad you didn't change your mind. You know, I really thought you were going to change your mind. I hope I didn't take up too much of your time.

ROSALIND: My time.

CASPAR: Right.

ROSALIND: To be honest I'm not sure anymore how terribly valuable my time is...Or maybe I haven't been...allotting it to the right things. I don't know.

CASPAR: You don't know?

ROSALIND: Well, I...

CASPAR: You're serious.

ROSALIND: I'm sorry—I shouldn't have said anything.

CASPAR: Haven't you heard the story about the woman physicist who had to sneak into Princeton's lab in the middle of the night to use the cyclotron? And you probably know women aren't even permitted into Harvard's physics building.

ROSALIND: Yes. I know that.

CASPAR: And yet here *you* are, doing this amazing...no, groundbreaking work. And still you aren't sure you're allotting your time correctly? I can't think of a better allotment of anyone's time.

ROSALIND: I don't know.

CASPAR: Well, I do.

> *A breath.*

ROSALIND: Should we get some tea then?

CASPAR: Rosalind...I have a confession. You might not like it.

ROSALIND: What?

CASPAR: I hate tea. I hate it. I mean, I really hate it. I can't even pretend to like it.

ROSALIND: Oh. Well, that is pretty bad. I think I'm rethinking everything I ever thought about you.

CASPAR: *(A genuine question.)* What did you think about me?

> *Beat. Awkward. Then, ROSALIND considers it.*

ROSALIND: *(Honestly, openly.)* I thought...you seemed balanced.

CASPAR: If by balance you mean always *about* to take a horrible misstep and have it all come crashing down around me, then maybe…

ROSALIND: No…See, I've never had a balance.

> *Beat.*

CASPAR: No?

ROSALIND: No.

CASPAR: But you've been happy.

> *A long beat—she is taken aback.*

ROSALIND: Of course.

> *Beat.*

Of course. Otherwise, why would I have…

CASPAR: Why would you have what?

ROSALIND: Continued on, I guess, in this way.

CASPAR: Right. You wouldn't have.

ROSALIND: Right.

CASPAR: You know, I have this theory…I think the things we want but can't have are probably the things that define us…And I've spent more time than I'd like to admit coming to this pretty simple conclusion so I hope you don't think it's completely ridiculous. But…I guess I'm talking about…I don't know…yearning?

ROSALIND: Yearning?

CASPAR: I mean…what do you want, Rosalind?

ROSALIND: So many things: to wake up without feeling the weight of the day pressing down, to fall asleep more easily, without wondering what it is that's keeping me awake, to eat more greens and also beetroot, to be kissed, to feel important, to learn how to be okay being with other people, and also how to be alone. To be a child again, held up and admired, the world full of endless future. To see my father look at me with uncomplicated pride. To be kissed. To feel every day what it would be to stand at the summit of a mountain in Wales, or Switzerland, or America, looking out over the world on a late afternoon with this man sitting across from me. Or to feel it once.

GOSLING: But instead she said:

ROSALIND: *(Sadly.)* I don't know.

CASPAR takes her hand.

CRICK: It's two strands. The bases go in the middle and the phosphates on the outside. It has to be.

WATSON: And we match the larger base with the smaller one.

They step back and look at the model they've created. Silence.

WATSON: Crick.

CRICK: Wait. Don't say anything.

WATSON holds up his sketch of Photograph 51; they look from sketch to model and back again.

CASPAR: Is this okay?

GOSLING: There's no science that can explain it. Loneliness.

ROSALIND looks down at her hand in his. The moment of possibility lingers. Then a strange look comes over her face.

CASPAR: Rosalind?

She clutches her stomach.

WATSON: It works, Francis. It works.

A very long beat.

CRICK: It's…

WATSON: I can't believe it.

CRICK: It's life unfolding, right in front of us.

ROSALIND doubles over in her chair, and gasps.

CASPAR: Rosalind?

WILKINS: It's the loneliest pursuit in the world. Science. Because there either are answers or there aren't. There either is a landscape that stretches before you or there isn't. And when there isn't, when you're left in the darkness of an empty city at night, you have only yourself.

CASPAR: I'll get you help. I'll bring you somewhere.

ROSALIND: A doctor.

CASPAR: Yes.

ROSALIND: Thank you.

CASPAR: Please don't thank me.

ROSALIND: Don't worry—I won't do it again. It wasn't easy for me.

Lights shift.

WILKINS: When they said they had something to show me, I had a feeling. All the way there on the train, the world seemed to move very quickly, as though passing me by.

He sees the model.

CRICK: Well?

WATSON: Say something, Wilkins.

ROSALIND: *(To the audience.)* I have two tumors. Twin tumors. Twins scampering around my body on tricycles, dropping handfuls of dirt as they go...For a moment I think of naming one Watson and the other Crick, but no, I tell myself: Rosalind, dispel the thought. *(Beat.)* No. I have ovarian cancer. A tumor in each ovary, one the size of a tennis ball, and the other a croquet ball, and they are indeed an efficient pair.

WATSON: You're really just going to stand there gaping? After all this?

CRICK: Let's have something at least. Come on. Give us something.

WILKINS: *(Resolutely.)* I think you're a couple of old rogues but you may well have something. I think it's a very exciting notion and who the hell got it isn't what matters.

WATSON: *(Matter-of-factly.)* An exciting notion? It's the secret of life, Wilkins.

WILKINS: *(Sadly.)* But is it? Is it *really,* Jim?

CASPAR: Rosalind, listen to me.

ROSALIND: Why? I'm not sure there is much else one could choose to see on those X-rays.

CASPAR: I'm going to find another hospital.

ROSALIND: Just go home, Don. I'm fine here.

CASPAR: How could you possibly think I'd leave you here all alone?

ROSALIND: But why would you stay?

CASPAR: Because I like you.

ROSALIND: *(Sadly; this isn't possibly enough.)* You like me.

> *He exits. The lights shift.*

WILKINS: Dear Miss Franklin.

No.

Rosalind.

No.

Dear Dr. Franklin: I was so sorry to hear about your illness. I'm sure you'll come out on the other side of it, however, and be back at King's in no time. Really, you haven't missed much. Things have been exceptionally dull around here. The equipment is getting dusty from disuse; it's been raining nonstop, of course; Watson and Crick discovered the secret of life. My teeth hurt in the mornings, just after I wake up. Dr. Randall sends his regards. We all miss you. No.

We trust you'll soon be well.

Yours, Maurice Wilkins.

> *Lights shift.*

WATSON: *(Holding up the copy of 'Nature'.)* Can you believe it, Crick? I mean, can you really believe it?

CRICK: I can't, I can't.

WATSON: Why do you seem so tired? I can't sit still. I'm energized. I want to take on everything now. The world. Everything. Women. You know.

CRICK: And you will.

WATSON: Crick?

CRICK: You will…I'm just tired, I think.

WATSON: But wasn't it worth it? Now we'll never be forgotten.

CRICK: Never.

WATSON: That's right.

CRICK: Never forgotten.

WATSON: Francis?

CRICK: Truly all I ever wanted was to support my family, to do science, to make some small difference in the world.

WATSON: Is it really so awful that you ended up making a big difference instead?

CRICK: Odile has taken the guest room as her own. She moved her things into it slowly, gradually, over the last few months. She was clever. It was only when nothing was left that I realized she was gone.

Lights shift. ROSALIND sees WILKINS in her office.

ROSALIND: Maurice, what are you doing here? Why on earth are you sitting in my office in the dark?

WILKINS: Oh—I'm so sorry; I thought you were still…

ROSALIND: *(Matter-of-factly.)* I escaped.

WILKINS: You—?

ROSALIND: I don't intend to spend any more time in that hospital. If I'm going to be in a dank, disgusting little room, I may as well be here, where I might even get some work done before I die.

WILKINS: Please don't say that.

ROSALIND: Why not? It's not pleasant? It makes you think about your own life? The inevitability of your own death?

WILKINS: Yes. All of those things.

ROSALIND: Well, no one can protect you from those.

WILKINS: No. No I suppose not.

ROSALIND: We lose. In the end, we lose. The work is never finished and in the meantime our bodies wind down, tick slower, sputter out.

WILKINS: Like grandfather clocks.

ROSALIND: Well this has been a pleasant conversation.

WILKINS: Rosalind, I…

Beat.

ROSALIND: When I was fifteen or sixteen, my family went on holiday to Norway. One morning, we woke at four and started up Storgalten…Mother couldn't stop complaining– it was too early, and too cold–until she looked around, that is. Because there we were, in the middle of a cloud. And we walked through it for what felt like an eternity, and there was no one else and there was no earth, no complicated history, no war about to unfold, just us, walking through this particular morning, watching the day begin.

At the time I told my father that I was moved by the natural beauty of our world: clouds–frozen crystals of ice suspended in the air, evaporating just before they hit the ground.

My father looked at me in a new way. He said yes that was true, but really we were seeing God–my father, who never believed. A man of science through and through. And when the sun rose, and the cloud lifted, we walked out onto the glacier, and he wept.

Beat.

WILKINS: You know…I've never felt the two have to be at odds.

ROSALIND: And yet they are intrinsically, unavoidably at odds.

Beat.

ROSALIND: So they really got it, did they? Our friends.

WILKINS: Yes.

ROSALIND: And is the model…is it just beautiful?

WILKINS: *(With real feeling.)* Yes.

ROSALIND: Well. We were close, weren't we? By god, we were close.

WILKINS: But we lost.

ROSALIND: Lost? No...We all won. The world won, didn't it?

WILKINS: But aren't you at all...

ROSALIND: Yes, but...It's not that they got it first...It really isn't...It's that I didn't see it. I wish I'd been able to see it.

WILKINS: I suspect you didn't allow yourself to see it...

ROSALIND: No, but with a little more time, I like to think I would have.

WILKINS: A few more days, even.

ROSALIND: So then why didn't I get those days? Who decided I shouldn't get those days? Didn't I deserve them?

> *Beat.*

I mean, if I'd only...

GOSLING: Been more careful around the beam.

WATSON: Collaborated.

CRICK: Been more open, less wary. Less self-protective.

CASPAR: Or more wary, more self-protective.

WATSON: Been a better scientist.

CASPAR: Been willing to take more risks, make models, go forward without the certainty of proof.

CRICK: Been friendlier.

GOSLING: Or born at another time.

CRICK: Or born a man.

ROSALIND: But you'll see. The work never ends. Next month I'm going to go to a conference in Leeds with one of my colleagues from Paris. We're going to drive there, stop off at some Norman churches along the way.

WILKINS: Churches?

ROSALIND: I do love the shapes of things, you know. I love them even before they mean something.

GOSLING: But she never went to Leeds. Rosalind was thirty-seven when she died. It was a particularly cold April that year; there was frost on the trees in London; the Alps stayed snow-covered well into June.

WILKINS: No, no, no…I won't have it.

GOSLING: Eulogies about her focused on her single-minded devotion to work, the progress she made in her work, the lasting contributions she made through her work.

WILKINS: *(To GOSLING.)* Stop that! I said: stop that right now.

GOSLING: I can't. It's what happened.

CASPAR: It's the tricky thing about time, and memory. I tell my grandchildren: whole worlds of things we wish had happened are as real in our heads as what actually did occur.

WILKINS: Stop that right now. We start again. At the beginning. This instant.

CRICK: Come on, old boy, don't you think enough is enough?

WILKINS: Not until we've gotten it right! We start again.

WATSON: You've gotta be kidding me, Wilkins. I mean, you won. We won. Your name on the Nobel Prize. Remember that part? For God's sakes: this was the finest moment in your life.

WILKINS: No. It wasn't.

> *He turns to ROSALIND.*

We start again. Just us this time.

WILKINS: *(Pleading with her, while the others exit.)* Please…You see, I need…

ROSALIND: *(Gently.)* What is it you need, Maurice?

WILKINS: There's something I need to tell you…It's important.

ROSALIND: Then tell me.

Beat.

WILKINS: I saw you. The day you went to see *The Winter's Tale* at the Phoenix.

ROSALIND: This is what you needed to tell me?

WILKINS: And I wanted to join you. I got in the queue to buy a ticket.

ROSALIND: All right, so what happened?

WILKINS: It's not what happened…It's what could happen. Now.

ROSALIND: What are you talking about, Maurice?

WILKINS: January, 1951. This time, I attend the play. And I see you across the theater.

He looks to her. She remains still, unmoved.

WILKINS: This time, we make eye contact. And afterwards, we meet in the back. By the bar.

She doesn't move.

WILKINS: This time I say, "did you enjoy the performance?"

She stares at him. Says nothing.

WILKINS: "Gielgud is excellent, don't you think?"

Beat.

ROSALIND: Yes, very lifelike. Very good.

WILKINS: And the incredible thing is we're both there, watching him. Experiencing the very same thing. Together.

ROSALIND: It is incredible.

WILKINS: Both watching.

ROSALIND: And when Hermione died, even though it was Leontes' fault, I felt for him. I truly did.

WILKINS: *Come, poor babe:*
I have heard, but not believed–

ROSALIND AND WILKINS: *The spirits o' the dead*
May walk again.

273

WILKINS: And they do. I love that Hermione wasn't really dead. That she comes back.

ROSALIND: *(Sympathetically.)* No, Maurice. She doesn't. Not really.

WILKINS: Of course she does.

ROSALIND: No.

WILKINS: Then how do you explain the statue coming to life?

ROSALIND: Hope. They all project it. Leontes projects life where there is none, so he can be forgiven.

WILKINS: But don't you think he deserves to be forgiven?

ROSALIND: Do I forgive myself?

WILKINS: What? For what?

> *Beat.*

ROSALIND: You know…I think there must come a point in life when you realize you *can't* begin again. That you've made the decisions you've made and then you live with them or you spend your whole life in regret.

WILKINS: And I have spent my whole life in regret.

> *Beat.*

ROSALIND: *(Smiling sadly.)* Well then perhaps we should have seen the play together.

Or gone to lunch.

WILKINS: Would that have changed things?

> *Long beat. She looks at him, decides to say something else.*

ROSALIND: It's strange, you know. That I can't remember who played Hermione.

WILKINS: No…I can't either. Not for the life of me.

ROSALIND: She simply didn't stand out, I suppose.

(With less conviction.) And that's that.

> *The lights slowly fade.*

Special thanks to

Billy Carden, Arthur Kopit, Linsay Firman, Seth Glewen, GT Upchurch, Danielle Mages Amato, Eric Louie, Barry Edelstein, Michael Grandage, James Bierman, Nicole Kidman, Daniella Topol, Braden Abraham, Shirley Serotsky, Ari Roth, Katherine Kovner, Kate Pines Kirschner, Michael Haney, Blake Robison, Jonathan Silverstein, Mark Armstrong, Andy Polk, Doron Weber, Simon Levy, Evan Cabnet, Mary Resing, Graeme Gillis, Erik Pearson, Margot Bordelon, Tamara Fisch, Jill Rafson and the fine folks at Oberon without whom this book would not exist: James Hogan, George Spender, Tia Begum and James Illman.

And, of course, my family:
Will, Elliot, David, Andrew, Bobby L. and Mom and Dad